Assertiveness Training

How to Stop People Pleasing and Caring What Others Think While Becoming More Assertive without Offending Others

© Copyright 2023 - All rights reserved.

The content contained within this book may not be reproduced, duplicated, or transmitted without direct written permission from the author or the publisher.

Under no circumstances will any blame or legal responsibility be held against the publisher, or author, for any damages, reparation, or monetary loss due to the information contained within this book, either directly or indirectly.

Legal Notice:

This book is copyright protected. It is only for personal use. You cannot amend, distribute, sell, use, quote, or paraphrase any part of the content within this book without the consent of the author or publisher.

Disclaimer Notice:

Please note the information contained within this document is for educational and entertainment purposes only. All effort has been executed to present accurate, up-to-date, reliable, and complete information. No warranties of any kind are declared or implied. Readers acknowledge that the author is not engaging in the rendering of legal, financial, medical, or professional advice. The content within this book has been derived from various sources. Please consult a licensed professional before attempting any techniques outlined in this book.

By reading this document, the reader agrees that under no circumstances is the author responsible for any losses, direct or indirect, that are incurred as a result of the use of the information contained within this document, including, but not limited to, errors, omissions, or inaccuracies.

Free Bonus from Andy Gardner

Hi!

My name is Andy Gardner, and first off, I want to THANK YOU for reading my book.

Now you have a chance to join my exclusive email list related to human psychology and self-development so you can get the ebook below for free as well as the potential to get more ebooks for free! Simply click the link below to join.

P.S. Remember that it's 100% free to join the list.

Access your free bonuses here:
https://livetolearn.lpages.co/assertiveness-training-paperback/

Table of Contents

INTRODUCTION 1
CHAPTER 1: UNDERSTANDING WHAT ASSERTIVENESS IS 3
CHAPTER 2: WHY ASSERTIVENESS CAN BE DIFFICULT 10
CHAPTER 3: HOW TO KILL THE PEOPLE-PLEASING MINDSET 20
CHAPTER 4: SETTING HEALTHY BOUNDARIES FOR YOURSELF 30
CHAPTER 5: SAYING NO WITHOUT FEELING GUILTY 43
CHAPTER 6: HOW TO NOT GIVE A D*MN (WHILE NOT BEING OFFENSIVE) 53
CHAPTER 7: 11 WAYS TO SHOW ASSERTIVENESS WITH BODY LANGUAGE 62
CHAPTER 8: SPEAK YOUR MIND WITHOUT APOLOGIZING 72
CHAPTER 9: DEALING WITH CONFLICT AND STANDING YOUR GROUND 81
CHAPTER 10: HOW TO BE ASSERTIVE IN DIFFERENT RELATIONSHIPS 89
CONCLUSION 98
HERE'S ANOTHER BOOK BY ANDY GARDNER THAT YOU MIGHT LIKE 100
FREE BONUS FROM ANDY GARDNER 101
REFERENCES 102

Introduction

As fundamental as it ought to be, assertiveness is not always a skill easy to acquire or develop, and people who lack it are often overlooked. If you feel that your ideas are not being heard or are dismissed, it's probably because you're nonassertive. You're either willing to go along with other people's opinions or fear expressing your own. While it's sometimes worth remaining passive, in most cases, it isn't. As you'll learn from this book, nonassertive behavior often leads to many issues, including aggressive outbursts followed by instant regret, whereas showing assertiveness without being rude or offensive has plenty of benefits. However, this is often easier said than done because your emotions rule your thoughts, and most of the time, these stop you from speaking your mind.

This book provides plenty of practical techniques to uncover the emotions behind nonassertive behavior. You'll also find various beginner-friendly exercises to overcome a people-pleasing mindset, yet another reason you may have trouble expressing your opinions. Wanting to preserve a relationship is very good, but not when it causes you to feel your needs aren't validated. One of the best ways to ensure your needs and opinions are validated is to set boundaries. Showing people how you expect them to behave in relationships with you is the perfect stepping stone toward learning to be assertive in different areas of your life.

Another issue discussed thoroughly in this book is saying no. Similar to going along with other people's opinions, saying no to their requests can be challenging because you may feel that by doing so, you'll seem pushy, offensive, and uncaring. However, being assertive isn't the same as being aggressive. Fortunately, there are some excellent ways to get around this, and you'll learn them from the relevant chapter. You'll also get the chance to identify the best ways to stop caring what other people think about you, your thoughts, and your actions.

Becoming assertive takes a lot of time and dedication. Through the last four chapters, you'll be introduced to even more practical techniques to implement assertiveness into your life - starting with your body language. Here you'll learn that it's just as crucial to leave a space as it is to govern a conversation by having a confident posture. This will help you back up your words whenever you decide to speak your mind. And most importantly, the techniques you'll learn will help you not feel guilty even when you firmly state your opinion during conflicts and arguments.

Lastly, you'll discover how to implement all the techniques you've learned about into different types of relationships and make these healthier and more balanced. By improving your communication style, you'll also become more productive in all areas of life and accomplish all the goals you set for yourself. If you're ready to embark on this journey and become more assertive, continue reading.

Chapter 1: Understanding What Assertiveness Is

Assertiveness is a highly desirable social skill – with plenty of benefits – and is used to create effective communication habits. However, before delving into the specifics of becoming assertive in your day-to-day life, you'll need to understand what this skill entails. This chapter discusses the concept of assertiveness and explains why demonstrating it is critical to living a productive life. Being assertive will empower you to stand up for your beliefs healthily, and this chapter will help you understand why.

Assertiveness is a crucial social skill.
https://unsplash.com/photos/lp1AKIUV3yo

What Is Assertiveness?

Regardless of the type of conversation you're having with someone, you always have the right to express your beliefs. However, to do that confidently, you must reassure yourself and others that what you're saying is relevant and not just a senseless comment. Presenting your thoughts in this way is called assertiveness. It's a positive trait because you'll know that your idea will be heard instead of dismissed.

Assertiveness is a set of skills that help people express their opinions and stand up for what they or others believe in. Assertive people always seem self-assured, bold, and unapologetic without being rude or offensive. Suppose you've ever come across a person who presented facts or opinions to a group of people and had their audience engrossed. In that case, this is probably thanks to assertiveness and confidence. Many think this only occurs in professional settings when someone makes a presentation to win support for a project or ace a job interview by showcasing their skills confidently. This isn't true because being assertive can come in handy in many other areas of your life.

Conversely, if their speech keeps getting interrupted, or they buckle to other people's ideas when asked a question, they are not being assertive. For example, maybe you're afraid to say no when a family member asks for help, thinking you'll offend them if you do. In this case, you're displaying nonassertive behavior. This means that assertiveness is also useful in replying to requests you don't want to or can't entertain.

Assertiveness, Passiveness, and Aggressiveness

Being nonassertive usually makes you a passive conversationalist. Sometimes, this can be a good thing. For instance, if your friend needs someone to listen to them vent about a personal issue, you may want to remain passive. However, this doesn't mean you can't express your opinion afterward or at any other time. Complying with the ideas and wishes of other people while disregarding your own thoughts is the opposite of being assertive. In these situations, your needs, rights, and the rights of the people you represent are undermined. For example, if you say yes when you want to say no, you're being passive or nonassertive. There's a clear difference between passiveness and assertiveness. Distinguishing the latter from aggressiveness is a little more challenging. Aggressive people refuse to consider other people's rights, but so do seemingly assertive people. However, there are some significant differences between these two behaviors. If someone keeps stating their opinions without considering other people's viewpoints, they're not being assertive. They're undermining everyone else's rights, which means they are showcasing aggressive behavior.

Different situations call for different approaches and dictate how you respond to people. In some cases, it can be more challenging to decide whether you should demonstrate assertiveness or not. However, if you have to choose between being assertive, passive, or aggressive, the first option is always the safest bet. It's always better to let people know where you stand firmly than to leave them guessing what you're thinking by remaining passive or leaving the wrong impression by being too aggressive.

Confidence and Other Traits

As mentioned before, assertive people are always confident. This is because they always tell the truth. Even if you're speaking your own truth, if you believe in it, you'll be able to present it assertively. If you don't acknowledge what you're saying as the truth, you'll have no chance of convincing others. One trait assertive people have in common is the ability to work hard for what they want. They haven't become as confident and successful as they are overnight. They practiced and honed their skills until they could use them to their benefit. They're not afraid to make mistakes during practice or live situations because they know their hard work will eventually pay off. They also realize patience is a virtue. By not rushing things, they'll make fewer mistakes. You'll have a much better chance of being heard if you speak slowly and with deliberate confidence because people will understand you.

That said, bold people are never overly confident. They know that they'll have to keep working on their assertiveness. Assertive people have weaknesses, too. They're just often very good at hiding them. You'll never catch them being nervous, even in the most challenging situations. They've learned to overcome whatever makes them nervous, or if they didn't, they make it seem like they did. Assertiveness also means that you're not afraid of what others will say, even if your opinions are unpopular or if you are in the company of unfamiliar people.

Assertiveness is keeping your emotional state in check. How can you sound assertive if you're anxious, frustrated, or upset most of the time? The answer is simple. You can't. And by not doing anything to get out of that state, you'll be stuck while all the assertive people around you make progress. Assertive people are good at keeping their emotions and the different aspects of their life separate from each other. For example, they often develop the ability to avoid mixing their professional life with their personal life. This makes them more productive in both areas because they can always focus on what's important. At work, they don't think about whatever issues they have with their partner at home. Because of this separation, their minds remain calm, and they can concentrate on being competent at their job.

Another common characteristic of assertive people is never losing faith in themselves, even in the most challenging circumstances. Let's say you've got an interview for a highly sought-after position and are competing against candidates who, on paper, have much better qualifications than yours. By being assertive, you can demonstrate your experience in the relevant field. You'll present yourself as a better candidate than all the others and get the position of your dreams.

Assertive people choose their words very carefully. They like to get to the point but will not blurt out whatever they want to say without thinking. They know that the audience needs a relevant context, but not so much that they lose interest. As mentioned before, they don't lie. If an assertive person doesn't know something, they are not afraid to say it. If they don't want to do something, they'll let this be known loudly and clearly and won't come up with lame excuses. This is another way to remain focused. The fewer lines of conversation you need to keep up with at any point in time, the more productive you'll become.

Assertiveness goes against people-pleasing behavior. People who know how to stand their ground do not worry about doing or saying things to maintain a good relationship with someone. They don't offer fake or nervous smiles to please others when discussing a serious topic. The latter can be particularly off-putting as people will know instantly that the person lacks confidence in their beliefs. Assertive people, on the other hand, understand how to assume the appropriate position and attitude. This makes people trust them even before they begin to speak.

Assertiveness also means being unapologetic. This doesn't mean assertive people spend their time thinking about hurting others. They're perfectly capable of remaining on top of things without this. They don't nurse emotions like jealousy or anger, which could feed a need to disrespect other people's rights. This is because they realize that if they give respect, they will receive the same kind of treatment.

And in the same way, they value their own space, time, and traits, so they also value that other people need that space. Another fundamental rule of assertiveness is that to be heard, you must first learn to listen. This way, you can learn what it takes to become an accepted and valued community member.

Why Is Assertiveness Important?

Being assertive has a broad range of benefits. For starters, it shows you're a confident person who isn't afraid to express your thoughts and feelings, regardless of how they may be received. Assertiveness is also linked to high self-esteem levels. If you're standing your ground, people will pick up that you control your thoughts, beliefs, emotions, and actions and won't let anyone else control them. Being assertive also shows that your well-being is important to you. You're being firm and decisive by not allowing other people to invade your personal space and constantly taking advantage of your time. You're signaling that these things are critical to you and that you care to use them for your own benefit. Being assertive is self-care. It cultivates self-love and self-awareness, qualities essential for personal growth.

Assertiveness portrays confidence and demands attention.
https://unsplash.com/photos/K0c8ko3e6AA

They're also great for keeping your mental health in check. Think about it this way: doesn't expressing your opinions and desires make you feel better about yourself? And doesn't keeping it all in just to keep peace in your relationships make you feel anxious, depressed, and devalued? You can save yourself a lot of headaches by becoming more assertive. With less anxiety, your mind will be free to work on more important things. Whether it's a new project at work, your relationship with your partner, or doing simple household chores, everything will become easier when you aren't haunted by second-guessing yourself.

What if, instead of helping my friend move, I finally took the time to clean my own home?

What if instead of constantly picking up the workload after a coworker and working overtime, I choose to dedicate that time to myself?

If you keep asking yourself questions like this, it's a clear sign that you must become more assertive.

Assertiveness can make you a better conversationalist. When you're being assertive, you clearly communicate your viewpoint and make your wishes known. At the same time, you're not demanding anything from others. You state your piece ensuring everyone will hear it, but you don't expect people to accept it as a fact. You leave them the choice to make up their own minds. Assertive people don't get angry when their needs aren't met. Regardless of how much work they put in trying to convince others that they deserve what they're asking for, they won't lash out. They move on and try to find a better way to express their needs and opinions and be even more assertive next time around. This ability enables them to stand up for themselves or others in a non-threatening way.

You'll have a much better chance of getting what you want if you're assertive. Let's say you ask your boss for a day off. If you're not assertive enough, they'll not believe that your reasons are valid and will probably say no. Whereas, if you put your foot down and clearly explain why you need the time off, you have much better chances of getting it.

When you learn to speak more assertively, you'll be able to escape the pitfalls of exhibiting passivity and nonassertive behavior. The negative emotions you can avoid by standing your ground include insecurity, fear, self-doubt, and other feelings brought on by self-defeating thoughts. Some people who fail to be assertive in their day-to-day lives are also exceptionally sensitive to criticism. On the other hand, those who are more assertive will take any criticism and either turn it into a learning opportunity or will know how to refute it right away. Either way, assertiveness can only help you become a better person. It will enable you to set smarter goals and reach them. Yet, despite being a fundamental skill for reaching goals, including personal growth and prosperity, being decisive and convincing doesn't come easy to many. In the next chapter, you'll learn more about why people struggle with demonstrating assertiveness, so make sure you continue reading.

Chapter 2: Why Assertiveness Can Be Difficult

Assertiveness isn't something that comes naturally to everyone. In fact, many people find it so difficult that they avoid any situation where it may be necessary. In 2022, 55% of adults reported that their lack of assertiveness had hampered their chances of promotion at work, according to Assertive Statistics and Facts. Understandably it can feel unnatural to be so upfront with how you feel and what you want from others. There are many reasons being assertive can be difficult for some people, and perhaps you've never been taught or allowed to practice it before. Maybe you're afraid of appearing too pushy, or it could be the people who matter most to you have a habit of pushing your boundaries and making you feel uncomfortable about expressing yourself. But why is this the case? This chapter will examine why assertiveness is so difficult and what a lack of assertion looks like.

Being assertive can be difficult for some people.
https://unsplash.com/photos/-Xv7k95vOFA

Why Assertiveness Can Be Difficult

As we all know, being assertive is a key skill everyone should have in their personal and professional arsenal. However, being assertive isn't always easy. In fact, many people struggle with this skill because they have trouble understanding why they aren't being as assertive as they would like. Several factors can stand in the way of assertive behavior. These include:

- A lack of self-esteem or confidence
- Fear of rejection or humiliation
- Lack of effective communication skills
- Lack of experience with assertive behavior
- Fear of confrontation and conflict
- Inability to cope with emotionally charged situations.
- Lack of trust in decision-making
- Worry about hurting the other person's feelings
- Fear of seeming too pushy or controlling

In addition to these, certain situations make it more difficult for someone to be assertive. For example, some people feel more comfortable being assertive in certain situations, while others find it easier to be quieter. There may also be other people around who influence the person's overall level of assertiveness. One way to overcome these issues is to become more aware of the factors that stand in the way of your assertiveness and work on them as necessary.

You Don't Know What Being Assertive Means

Putting a label on your inability to stand up for yourself is quite challenging. When "assertiveness" is mentioned, most people imagine someone loudly standing up for themselves. But this isn't always the case. Being assertive doesn't mean yelling your point across the room or storming out of a meeting. Rather, it means speaking confidently while maintaining composure and respect. If you aren't sure of what assertiveness means, you'll most likely adopt passive communication, which is one of the most common unassertive communication styles. Passive communication is characterized by a lack of directness, a focus on feelings, and a desire to avoid conflict. Being passive isn't necessarily the same as being unassertive, but passive people often find it difficult to express their feelings directly, which is a key aspect of being assertive.

Your Flight or Fight Response Is Activated

Flight or fight is a term used to describe a stress response. In this state, the body's autonomic nervous system is activated. This system is responsible for regulating and controlling the body's activities, and when a stressful situation occurs, these controls are activated to help the body prepare for a difficult situation. The most likely reactions include:

- Increased heart rate
- Muscle tension
- Increased breathing rate
- Sweating
- Blinking rate

These are all typical stress symptoms. A flight or fight response is when you feel threatened by an incoming situation and react by either running away (flight) or fighting back (fight). Many people with anxiety are more likely to use flight as a means to avoid conflict or manage their fear. When assertiveness is required, and stress symptoms kick in, you cannot regulate your stress and avoid uncomfortable situations if you are afraid to assert yourself. This is an unhealthy solution to stress; avoidance, defensiveness, and silence will not improve anything.

Your Emotions Get the Better of You

In this context, emotion clouds our judgment and makes us act in a way we would not necessarily act otherwise. You might feel angry, scared, or ashamed when you want to speak up for yourself, or if you do, you end up saying something you'll regret. When emotions are strong, you might feel that it is too risky to take a stand because assertiveness could be misinterpreted when you feel pressured or angry. This is another misconception about assertive behavior. People think that it is a sign of aggression to be assertive because it can be seen as a challenge to another person's authority. This isn't necessarily the case, though. When you're assertive, you're not challenging authority. You're just speaking up. If someone is controlling or abusive, then assertiveness can definitely be used to stand up for yourself.

You Feel Inferior or Worry about Being Obnoxious

Unassertive people are often anxious about saying the wrong thing or being critical of others. This is because they are afraid of the consequences. This is true for those in senior roles too. You worry about your performance being criticized, feeling inadequate, and being rejected by the people you work with.

Unassertive people are afraid of being disliked, so they put the needs of others before their own. They are more sensitive to criticism and worry more about upsetting people. Being unassertive can lead you to feel resentful, ashamed, and anxious. You may feel disappointed in yourself for not speaking up for what you deserve.

You Have a Fear of Rejection and Negative Outcomes

Rejection is a scary and uncomfortable experience for most people. It can make us feel vulnerable, exposed, and afraid. When we are too close to a fear of rejection, we can be prevented from asserting ourselves and taking control of a situation. This fear is often based on our past experiences of being rejected. Suppose we have been rejected or bullied in the past. In that case, that fear can become a subconscious reaction that we hold on to, which colors our future interactions with others unless we actively do something to heal ourselves. This fear can lead us to avoid challenging authority figures and speaking up for ourselves if it means rejection or criticism.

You may be afraid of the consequences if you tell your boss that you must take time off for an important family event.

- Maybe you're afraid of being rejected if you ask someone out
- You may notice that you feel anxious before going into situations in which you may be rejected by others
- Or maybe you dread speaking up at work because you're worried about making a mistake or looking foolish in front of your colleagues

You're Overthinking

If you're unassertive, you could be overthinking every situation and take longer to make decisions. You become so concerned with the details of a situation that you can't see the bigger picture. This paralyzes you, and you then feel even more fear that you can't or haven't made the right decision. Overthinking can lead you to be more passive because you're focused on the potential negative outcomes of making a decision. When you're afraid to make mistakes, you allow other people to make decisions for you.

You Are Insecure

When you feel insecure, you are likely to fear rejection or judgment from others. You also worry that people will think less of you if you are assertive. This can make it difficult to speak up when you disagree with someone or when your boss asks you to do something new. Another problem with feeling insecure is that it makes it hard to make decisions. When you feel uncertain about what to do, it can be tempting to follow the crowd and avoid taking risks. But this is not a good idea because everyone's opinion is not equal, and some people may have very good ideas while others don't. Finally, insecurity can lead to a lack of trust in others. If you do not trust other people, it will be much more difficult for them to trust you and your opinions.

You Have Low Self-Worth

Low self-worth can make it difficult to be assertive because you are less likely to speak up for yourself and more likely to take criticism personally. This can lead to passive behavior, where you don't stand up for your own needs or speak up when someone in authority is mistreating you. Some people with low self-worth can have difficulty knowing when they should speak up or back off from an interaction. It can also be difficult for them to understand that their feelings are valid and that they deserve respect. Those who are low on self-worth have a difficult time seeing themselves as capable and deserving of respect. This can make it difficult to know how to respond when someone belittles you, insults you, or treats you unfairly. These feelings make assertiveness difficult because you are less likely to be confident in your position or willing to stand up for yourself.

You're Afraid of Change

While everyone has some fear of change, some people are much more sensitive to it than others. This fear makes them reluctant to initiate changes in their lives and even more resistant to additional changes when they attempt to make them. When we fear what might happen if we go against the status quo, it's very easy to avoid taking risks and sticking our necks out for fear of being seen as a threat to the existing order.

You've Had Negative Past Experiences

The world is a complex place full of opportunities, challenges, and other people. When we're young, we're constantly learning about our environment. As we grow, we gain new experiences that help us develop skills and gauge our level of competence. These experiences can be positive or negative, but they all shape our self-confidence.

In adulthood, certain situations can trigger past experiences with assertive behavior.

To measure assertiveness, a study published in *Psychology of Women Quarterly* (2019) assessed 101 men and 113 women aged 20-60 and discovered that those who had studied at higher education institutions were more assertive than those who didn't. For example, an employee who did well in college will feel more confident making requests at work than someone who struggled with basic reading comprehension. They may also feel more comfortable asking for a raise or promotion than someone who received poor grades in high school or college. When these past experiences are negative and affect your self-confidence, it can be difficult to be assertive and take charge of your life.

You're Afraid of Appearing Selfish

A common misunderstanding about assertiveness is that it means being selfish and self-centered. Many people equate assertiveness with being rude, aggressive, or having an ego the size of Texas. Unfortunately, this misconception can make people who are socially anxious feel like they have no other option than to bottle up their feelings and hide away from the world. But the truth is, assertiveness is not about being rude or aggressive as it's about being honest and open with yourself and others. And while being honest and open may sometimes feel a little uncomfortable, it also feels good to be able to be yourself in a world where everyone else seems to be living someone else's life. So, if you want to start practicing more assertive behaviors, don't let these misconceptions keep you from getting started.

You Think Your Needs Don't Matter

Sometimes we don't realize how much power we actually have over our lives. We tend to think that it is other people - or the world in general - who are making decisions, and so we don't think we can change anything. This common misconception can result in frustration and anger when we finally decide to assert ourselves, only to see things not change. The truth is that no one else is in control of your life but you, and it's up to you to take action and make things happen for yourself. So, if you want something to change, start taking responsibility for your actions. Once you accept this, you'll likely feel empowered and ready to take action.

What Fear of Assertion Looks Like in a Situation

Now you know why assertiveness can be difficult, here are a couple of scenarios to give you a better idea of what it looks like.

In a Relationship

Fear of assertion is probably the most common fear in relationships. It's a fear of letting your partner know what you want from the relationship, and it's normally rooted in self-doubt and insecurity. It can manifest in many different ways, though.

For example, your partner keeps leaving wet towels around the house after a shower. As they've been having a tough time at work lately, they snap at you, and you don't want to add to their stress. Because you don't say anything, you spend a lot of time picking them up - but you also have your own things to do. It may sound trivial, but over time this situation can cause resentment.

Here are a few other situations:

- You worry that your needs are too big or too demanding, and so you shy away from asking for what you want. This fear could also come from the fear of rejection if you ask your partner for something that seems too big or too far out of reach.
- You think asking for more will lead to conflict and resentment, which could end up hurting the relationship in other ways.

That's why some people bury their heads in the sand and hope things will magically work out without ever taking action. This is actually a very unhealthy way to approach it, though.

In the Workplace

When you lack assertiveness in the workplace, you're likely to avoid difficult situations and questions, which can lead to problems in the long run.

For example, say you have been given a large project to complete. You're already stressed from an overwhelming workload as it is. A few members of your team have called in sick, which your boss is aware of. You know that if you take on this project, you'll have to work overtime and work on the weekend to complete it. You have a busy personal schedule to deal with too. Instead of reminding your boss that there are too few employees to complete the task, you don't say anything. And stretch yourself too thin in the process.

Other ways that a lack of assertiveness can show up in the workplace include:

- Hesitance to speak up in meetings or give feedback because you're not comfortable taking on leadership roles
- Always asking for help or favors because you're not confident in your abilities

What Fear of Assertion Looks Like Physically

You can use the chart below to examine your behavior, then use the quiz-style checklist below to determine how assertive you are (or aren't).

	Assertive	Submissive	Aggressive
Body Language	Maintaining eye contact Good posture Face to face	Lack of eye contact Arms wrapped around the body Lowered shoulders	Flailing hand gestures Intense eye contact Getting too close

	Assertive	Submissive	Aggressive
Tone of Voice	Direct and respectful	Intonation at the end of sentences	Angry, rude
Voice Volume	Solid and full	Quiet	Shouting / loud

Checklist

Use this checklist to assess whether you find it difficult to be assertive. Asking and answering these questions will give you a clear picture of what you need to do and whether you are on track. If you answer yes to any of these questions, you have difficulties asserting yourself.

1. I don't like to accept compliments from others because it means that I am arrogant.
2. Easygoing people don't make a fuss about things, so I should just take it as it comes.
3. There is no need for people to share their feelings with others.
4. Because I am unsure what I want, I will wait to see what others prefer, and then I will make up my mind.
5. People will dislike me if I tell them what I really think.
6. I'll come across as rude or selfish if I say what I really want.
7. I don't need to tell others what I really think or feel because those close to me should already know.
8. People disagree with me or tell me no because they don't really like me or love me.
9. If I stand up for myself, the other person will be upset, and our relationship will suffer.
10. If I speak up, I am afraid of causing a scene or drawing attention to myself.
11. I'm not allowed to change my mind.
12. Other people will be annoyed if I change my mind.

13. People will think I am incompetent if I admit I am feeling stressed or overburdened.
14. I don't want to burden others with my true feelings.
15. In any case, if I try to speak for myself, I will sound like an idiot, so what's the point?

Being unassertive means you're likely to put other people's needs before yours. It can affect your relationships at work and at home, and it can make you feel like a less confident and empowered person. If you want to become more assertive, you first have to understand what it means. Then, you have to remember that the other person is human, too, and you have the right to speak up for yourself.

Knowing why you're not assertive will help you to understand where your issues are coming from. As long as you can identify the source of your difficulties, you'll be able to take steps to rectify the situation and become more assertive. In essence, learning about the reasons behind your lack of assertiveness can help you understand what is going on under the surface and resolve any underlying issues.

Having learned why being assertive can be challenging, continue reading to learn how you can stop people pleasing to express what you really want.

Chapter 3: How to Kill the People-Pleasing Mindset

People-pleasing is a personality trait that describes someone with a strong need to please others. People-pleasers sacrifice their own needs, inconvenience themselves, and go above and beyond for others. Being liked is a people-pleaser's main purpose. Their own needs, happiness, and comfort aren't among their priorities. While it is normal to care about other people's feelings and be there for those in need, people-pleasers take it a step too far. They don't know how to say no and will do things they are uncomfortable about just to get validation from other people. This behavior can seem out of control as people-pleasers can't stop themselves. They will go to the extent of changing their personality and opinions and hide their true feelings if it makes others love them. People-pleasers can feel happy and good about themselves when they receive gratitude from others. However, this feeling is temporary, and eventually, they will feel the impact of this harmful behavior over time. It can make you lose your voice and feel that you don't have time for yourself since you devote all your time and energy to others. In severe cases, you lose your own identity as well.

People pleasing is a personality trait that may need to be controlled.
https://unsplash.com/photos/23KdVfc395A

Although people-pleasing can come from a good place, there is a deeper reason behind this desire to sacrifice your happiness for others. This chapter will help you determine whether you are a people-pleaser and explain the behavior associated with people-pleasing, as well as how you can kill this behavior and end it for good. Prepare yourself for an exciting journey in the mindset of a people-pleaser.

Why Am I a People-Pleaser?

You have probably asked yourself this question before, "Why do I care so much about pleasing people?" Fear can drive this behavior, whether it is fear of rejection or fear of abandonment. For instance, in relationships, some people put their partners' needs above their own and change their opinions and values to agree with their partner. They do this because they believe their partner will leave them if they aren't constantly agreeable and catering to their partner's needs. These relationships end up being one-sided, with one person doing all the giving, which can make the people-pleaser miserable. Fear of disappointment can also make a person eager to please. For instance, you have a back problem, and your doctor tells you to stay in bed for a week. A friend calls you to ask you to drive them to the airport, and out of fear of disappointing them, you agree and risk your own health.

However, if your friend really cares about you, they will understand that you are unwell.

According to psychologist Dr. Elena Touroni, people-pleasing behavior can begin in childhood. Children with people-pleasing parents grow up copying their parents' behavior. Dominating parents can influence their children to become people-pleasers as well. Business coach Iveta Zaklasnikova adds that people-pleasing is in our nature. Since ancient times, people felt safe being in groups as it was necessary for their survival. The need to be liked is part of people's nature as it makes them feel part of a group.

Other reasons behind people-pleasing behavior are:
- Worrying about what others think of you
- Lack of self-love
- A desire to fit in
- Saying no makes you feel guilty
- You are empathetic to others' needs to the extent that you end up taking care of everyone while forgetting about yourself

Am I a People-Pleaser?

Certain behaviors are associated with people-pleasing and can help give you an answer on whether you are a people-pleaser or not and which behaviors you display.

Being Agreeable

Giving people the space to share their opinion is good manners but agreeing with everything they say, even if you aren't convinced, is people-pleasing. Your desire to be liked and to please everyone can drive you to do or say things that make you uncomfortable. For instance, you have a job interview the next morning, but your friends want to go out drinking. Instead of telling them you can't come, you agree to go with them and risk going to the interview hungover.

Being Conflict-Shy

According to therapist Laura Steventon, people-pleasing is a protection mechanism some of us turn to avoid conflict. To avoid confrontations, you don't express your feelings, contradict others, or disagree with them. While it is natural to want to avoid conflict, you can't do that at your own expense. Conflicts are normal and can lead to a healthy conversation instead of going along with everything people say.

Having Difficulty Saying No

Do you find yourself saying "yes" to everything people tell you? People-pleasers can't say no because they don't want to disappoint others or are afraid of rejection. You either say yes and end up doing something you are uncomfortable with, or you come up later with an excuse to avoid this commitment. For instance, your friends invite you to a dinner party, but you don't feel like going. You agree to go when they invite you but later call and tell them that your child is sick and you can't come.

This quality is the biggest telltale sign that you are a people-pleaser. The inability to say no to anyone, even strangers, indicates your uncontrollable urge to please.

Feeling Stressed or Overwhelmed

Putting others first can lead to feelings of stress and overwhelm. Being there for everyone else drains your energy and keeps you exhausted. You give all your time and energy to others without sparing a moment to look after the only person that matters most - you. Ignoring your needs for the sake of others can damage your mental health. Not having "me" time or arranging your schedule based solely on others' wants and needs is stressful.

Being Passive Aggressive

People-pleasing and passive aggression are connected. Both behaviors result from fear of rejection and an eagerness to please. People-pleasers keep their feelings to themselves either to avoid confrontation or because they are afraid of disappointing others. Passive aggressive behavior can stem from hiding your true feelings, and it shows up in the form of sarcasm, cynicism, or resentment.

Being Prone to Resentment

People-pleasers suppress their anger when others take advantage of them or violate their boundaries. Even though they are eager to please, subconsciously, they feel resentment. For instance, your college roommate asks you to help her with research. You have an exam tomorrow, but you decide to give her a hand instead. You fail your exam while she manages to get extra credit. You can't help but feel resentment as she advances while you fail. You also feel angry at yourself for neglecting your own needs. Consider this resentment a wake-up call telling you it's time to change your behavior.

Being Quick to Take the Blame

Instead of standing up for themselves, people-pleasers are the first to take the blame, even for things that aren't their fault. Constantly apologizing rather than speaking up is a better option for people-pleasers who dread confrontation. Taking the blame is easier than explaining or defending yourself and risking people disliking you. You feel like everything is your responsibility, even other people's emotions – which makes you apologize for how they are feeling even when it has nothing to do with you.

Having Trouble Being True to Your Own Beliefs

Constantly agreeing with others can lead you to give up your own beliefs. For instance, you are sitting with friends from work, and they make fun of one of your co-workers who is devastated because he just got fired. Even though you find it harsh that they make fun of someone going through a tough time, you play along to please your friends and fit in with them.

How to Stop People-Pleasing Behavior

Being a people-pleaser isn't associated with kindness or compassion. You can still be a good person who helps others without sacrificing your own needs or principles. Understand that your family and friends will not cut you off if you disagree with them or say no. However, if anyone in your life makes you feel guilty when you don't put them first, these people are toxic, and you should set boundaries with them. People-pleasing isn't a disorder. It is a personality trait. Like any personality trait, persistence and hard work can help you to be more assertive and rid yourself of this bad habit. This part of the chapter will provide you with effective tips to help you stop people-pleasing.

How to Kill People-Pleasing Trait

Getting rid of any negative trait requires you to first acknowledge that you have a problem. Once you admit this to yourself, you should believe in your ability to change. Personality traits aren't set in stone. You can change them. According to a study conducted at the University of Houston, Texas, people's feelings, thoughts, and personality traits can change over time, and this change is usually for the better. Psychologist Dr. Benjamin Hardy conducted his own research on personality change as well. He found that personality traits are fluid. They are acquired due to the experiences and decisions one makes along the way. Hardy's research also concluded that a person can change their negative personality traits and beliefs with strong will and effort. Killing this trait is one decision away.

People-Pleasing Is a Choice

No one is making you a people-pleaser. You choose to act this way. You have probably been a people-pleaser for a long time, and it has become second nature. However, you have the power to stop. Change will only come when you know you have a choice instead of denying the problem. Be mindful and aware of people-pleasing behavior. Focus on your thoughts and reactions to better understand yourself and this trait instead of giving an automatic response. When you become self-aware, you will notice when you are pleasing others and acting differently.

Define Your Priorities

Set your priorities. Make a list of the significant people in your life, the ones you want to help. Next, set clear goals for yourself and decide where you want to be in life. Identifying your priorities will allow you to be selective about the people and things you are willing to give your time and energy. Be aware of the ones who drain your energy or manipulate you, and take the necessary actions. Say no and set boundaries for the things and people that don't align with your goals and priorities. Don't allow others to take time and energy that you can use to focus on yourself, help you achieve your goals, and spend time with the people that matter.

Don't Take the Blame

Stop apologizing for things that aren't your fault. Understandably, you want to be polite and considerate of other people's feelings. However, unnecessary apologies stem from your desire to please and be liked. Before apologizing, ask yourself, "Is this my fault?" "Did I make a mistake?" For instance, your friend's car broke down, and you recommend your mechanic for them. However, the mechanic took a large amount of money and couldn't fix the car. You want to say you are sorry because this is your mechanic, but this isn't your fault. You merely made a suggestion. You aren't to blame because they had a bad experience. Sympathize with them but apologizing is unnecessary.

Set Clear Boundaries

Setting boundaries will protect your mental health, time, and energy. It isn't selfish or cruel to have a line that people shouldn't cross. Boundaries will help you tell the difference between those who care about and respect you and those who take advantage of you. Setting healthy boundaries will be discussed in detail in the next chapter.

Learn to Say No

People-pleasers struggle with the word no. When faced with an uncomfortable situation, they use words like "I will try to make it" or "I will see what I can do." Saying "no" makes people uncomfortable, especially people-pleasers. Remember, every time you say yes at your own expense, you are saying no to yourself, and you end up neglecting your own needs. Transitioning from yes to no can be hard at first. People-pleasers have the need to be liked, and they have always associated no with being rude or insensitive. Instead of saying no right away, find a polite way to reject requests, like saying, "Thank you for inviting me, but I am very busy next weekend," or "I am flattered that you came to me first, but I have to pass." Other effective methods in the book will help you say no without feeling guilty.

No Is a Full Sentence

You don't owe anyone an explanation. If you are uncomfortable with something, just say no. Don't give excuses or explain your reasons. No is a full sentence. You don't have to follow it with anything else. Making excuses will invite people to come up with solutions or pressure you to change your decisions. For instance, a friend texts you, "Let's hang out tonight." You had a long day at work, the car is at the mechanic, and you want to relax at home. If you give your friend these excuses, they will offer to come to pick you up and convince you to go out instead of staying at home doing nothing. Texting them, "I can't tonight, maybe next weekend," is a polite way to say no and set boundaries. There are other situations when you can just say no, like when a friend offers you a drink while trying to stay sober. Here you can say "no," end of a sentence.

Give Yourself More Time

Give yourself some time before you decide whether to say yes or no. When a friend calls to invite you to something or asks you for a favor, don't respond right away. Take your time to gather more information and think things through before you commit to any obligations. Committing to something you don't want to do will leave you stressed and resentful. Buy yourself some time by saying, "Let me check if I have other plans and get back to you" "I may be working this weekend; I will call you if I can make it." During this time, consider whether this is something you'll enjoy or stress you out or whether you have the time.

Setting a Time Limit

Helping other people doesn't mean inconveniencing yourself. Set a time limit to prevent people from walking over you, and make it clear that your time and needs matter too. For instance, if you have a meeting in ten minutes and your sibling calls you, let them know that you'll have to hang up in a few minutes. Or if you are out with friends, make it clear that you have to get home early because you have a job interview the next day. Setting a time limit will give you more control over your life and empower you.

Recognize the Manipulators

Others are aware of your people-pleasing behavior and will take advantage of it. Recognize the difference between the genuine people who want your help and the manipulators who are using you. Some people use flattery to get you to do something for them. They can make it sound like a "genuine" compliment, but it's only to cover their true intentions. For instance, your sister-in-law's birthday is coming up, but your brother doesn't want to take an hour out of his day to shop for gifts. He calls you and says, "You have always had better taste than me, and you know that I am very busy. I know that she would love whatever you choose for her because you always put so much thought into your gift, unlike your idiot brother." Or a co-worker tricks you into doing their work for them by saying that you are much smarter than them or that you are an expert in this topic. When someone genuinely wants help, they will be straightforward yet ask nicely without the need for excessive flattery.

Repeat Mantras

Mantras are powerful and can help alter your thoughts. Create helpful mantras, write them on sticky notes, and hang them on your bathroom mirror so you can see them first thing in the morning, or set one as your phone wallpaper. Mantras can serve as a daily reminder that you have power over your decisions and reactions.

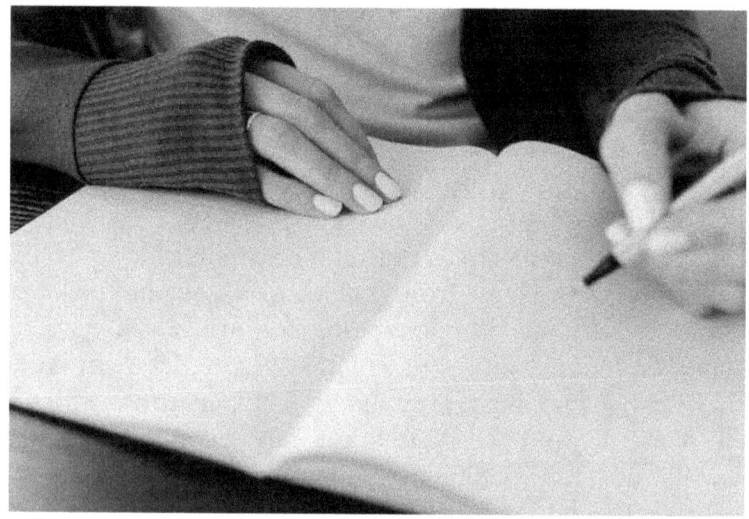

Making notes of your mantras can be helpful in organizing your thoughts.
https://unsplash.com/photos/xcvXS6wDCAY

Here are some mantras suggestions:
- I am in control of my energy and time
- I have the right to say *no*
- I can say *no* without an explanation
- *No* is a full sentence
- I don't take responsibility for other people's feelings
- Saying *no* sets me free

Embrace Positive Self-Talk

People-pleasing often stems from negative thoughts and insecurity. Replace these thoughts with positive ones by repeating powerful mantras or thinking positive thoughts that can help change your thought patterns. Remind yourself that your friends and family love you for who you are, not for what you do for them. Tell yourself you matter to the people in your life and that they love you even when you don't always do things for them or agree with them. Your self-worth isn't tied to what people think of you. You determine your worth.

Find the Root of Your People-Pleasing Behavior

Dig deep to understand the reason behind this behavior. Is it fear of abandonment? Is it fear of rejection? Do you have the need to be liked? Understand your feelings are valid, and you have the right to them. Analyze these feelings and get to their root. This can be tough, but recognizing these feelings can deprive them of their power. Therapy can help you here.

See a Therapist

Therapy is effective in helping people change negative personality traits. A good therapist will also help you uncover the main reason behind the people-pleasing behavior to work on your healing. They can also teach you effective methods to say no and set boundaries.

You can change. People-pleasing is hurting your mental health and affecting your well-being. It makes you stressed, overwhelmed, and keeps taking up your time and energy. A people-pleaser loses their identity along the way as their thoughts, opinions, and actions become a reflection of others.

Setting boundaries is one of the most effective ways to protect yourself and your own personal space. Once you experience the empowering feeling of boundaries, you'll never go back. Are you eager to step into the world of healthy boundaries and find out how to make others respect your needs? Turn to the next chapter, and start setting boundaries.

Chapter 4: Setting Healthy Boundaries for Yourself

Unfortunately, our boundaries are less visible to people than walls or huge "Do not enter" signs. They are more akin to invisible bubbles.

Boundaries represent the constraints to which we must all adhere. Setting and maintaining personal boundaries can be difficult, but it is necessary for your happiness, health, and safety. Having clear limits helps people feel in control of their environment, bodies, and emotions.

Setting boundaries helps you gain control.
https://unsplash.com/photos/DRzYMtae-vA

Learning to take control of your life by setting your own and respecting the boundaries of others cannot be taught by a textbook, but it can be practiced. You can use the guidelines in this chapter to set boundaries with loved ones or to protect your personal space when meeting new people.

Healthy Boundaries: What Are They?

You can take charge of your life when you establish boundaries. These are the limits you place on yourself to protect your feelings, body, time, thoughts, and mental well-being and to maintain your strength, stability, and happiness. These protective barriers keep others from abusing, draining, or manipulating you.

Some Possible Boundaries You May Want to Consider

Everyone has their constraints. Your boundaries will not be identical to those of anyone else because they should represent your unique requirements and objectives. However, this checklist may help you decide where to draw the line on personal restrictions.

You can set limits on the following:

- Psychological energy
- Time
- Finances and luxury items
- Private space
- Sexuality
- Principles and morals
- Social networking sites

Boundaries may be established with the following:

- Family
- Neighbors
- Romantic relationships
- Fellow employees
- Strangers

Why Do You Need Personal Boundaries?

Boundaries make it easier to set limits for yourself and establish positive life routines. They prevent you from engaging in unhealthy behaviors such as eating hamburgers at every meal or staying up until 1:00 a.m. when you have to be at work at 7:00 a.m.

To create them, you must draw parallels between what you consider acceptable and what you find unacceptable. This is your limit.

As an act of self-love and self-respect, we protect ourselves by establishing boundaries, and they preserve our safety and well-being. They ensure that our daily routines run smoothly.

The Challenges of Establishing Personal Boundaries

Despite our shared understanding of the benefits of discipline and organization, we all struggle to keep them. Have you considered the factors that make it so difficult for you to set limits on your actions? Some of the reasons that controlling your behavior seems so difficult are discussed below:

- Neither of your parents had a solid foundation of personal limitations and boundaries
- You lacked stable, acceptable boundaries and limits because your parents never established them
- Constraints and boundaries may make you feel suffocated and restricted
- Addiction and other mental illnesses can make it difficult to exercise self-control and cause cognitive problems

If you were fortunate, your parents instilled in you the importance of regular hygiene practices, such as brushing your teeth and going to bed on time. You have gradually internalized these rules and now use them to guide your behavior.

You now feel more secure because of everything you've learned about limitations. You now understand the importance of self-care and how to implement these ideas in your daily life.

Many of us, however, were raised by parents who lacked restrictions. You may find it difficult to establish healthy boundaries for yourself if you have never been taught the importance of doing so or if no one has ever explained why they are essential for your well-being.

Creating personal boundaries is one method of re-parenting yourself. Boundaries give you the safety and structure that you lacked as a child.

How to Establish Healthy Boundaries

Have you ever been made to feel uneasy or overworked by others? It's possible that someone simply crossed your boundary without you realizing it.

Here are some pointers on how to set your limits confidently:

Be Self-Assured

Setting boundaries with confidence makes one feel both strong and compassionate toward others. Communicating assertively means being clear and firm without demeaning or threatening the other person.

The "I" statement allows you to be assertive. It demonstrates self-assurance and excellent boundary-setting skills by expressing thoughts, feelings, and opinions without regard for what others may think.

For example, you could say, "When you read my diary, I feel my privacy has been violated. Instead of "Don't touch my diary!" or saying, "When every second of our trip is planned, I begin to feel stressed. Instead of "You're making this trip tiresome."

These two statements are excellent examples of how to use the "I" statement.

Understand When to Say No

"No" is a complete sentence, even though it's hard to say it sometimes. We may be hesitant to respond negatively without providing additional information, but this is unnecessary.

Setting boundaries does not always require confidence. Sometimes, all that is needed is a willingness to tolerate some discomfort on your part. A simple "no" does not require justification or any personal resonance on the part of the person you are rejecting.

You have every right to politely decline requests for your mobile number or a dance. If a coworker asks you to cover their shift and you refuse, you are not required to explain why.

Safeguard Your Space

You may also impose restrictions on your possessions, physical and mental space, time, and other resources without announcing them.

This could be done in a number of ways, one of which is by changing your strategy. Remember that periodic disengagement is necessary. The simple expectation of being reachable via email outside of normal business hours is enough to diminish your well-being and personal strain relationships. Create limits for work-life balance wherever possible.

When it comes to technology, an increasing number of couples are concerned about invading one another's privacy. Due to technological advancements, there has been a rapid loss of personal space and control.

As an individual, you are responsible for protecting your own devices and online activity and preventing any of your private communications from becoming public. It is essential that we all get used to discussing technological limitations with new friends and romantic partners.

Seek Support or Help

Setting and maintaining healthy boundaries may be more difficult if you or someone you care about struggles with mental health issues, depression, stress, or a traumatic past.

For example, a victim of sexual assault may expect to be asked first before being touched. A grown child of a narcissist or someone with a borderline personality disorder may need to learn how to say "no" to their emotionally fragile parent in a firm manner.

Never be afraid to seek the assistance of a psychotherapist if you are having difficulty creating or enforcing barriers or if another person is causing you stress by violating them.

Smart Boundary Protections

- Keep personal items in a secure cabinet
- Instead of a physical journal, keep a digital one that requires a password

- Prepare ahead of time to be completely alone or to act independently of others
- Use a password, PIN, or another method to secure your electronic equipment and online accounts
- Establish a deadline for responding to messages or emails
- Leave an "out of office" message on your email while you're away
- Send your application for the vacation ahead of time for approval
- If you do not want to be reached, temporarily disable your email and chat applications
- Put your phone and other electronic devices on silent mode
- Try to ignore any business-related communications sent to your personal accounts

How to Strike a Work-Life Balance

When there is no clear distinction between work and personal life, anxiety and stress increase, this is more important than ever, given the massive increase in telecommuting and home offices. Workaholism has become prevalent and manifests itself in a variety of ways, which must be acknowledged.

For example, Adam is a police officer with a strong work ethic and a track record of success. Unfortunately, he frequently spends too much time at his office, where he obsessively checks his computer and files at the expense of spending time with his family. He is anxious and preoccupied with cases from the moment he wakes up until the moment he falls asleep.

Adam jokes about being a "workaholic," but he really sees his job as an extension of himself. His cognitive, psychological, and physical well-being are all deteriorating due to his inability to separate work and personal life.

How to Stop Being a Workaholic and Start Living Your Life

- Keep your working hours consistent (it could be 9 to 4 with an hour break)
- Establish a self-care routine
- Keep your phone out of sight while spending time with loved ones
- Inform your colleagues and employees when you are unavailable
- Create a work-only area in your home
- Delegating responsibilities or adding more personnel may help alleviate stress
- Find something to do outside of work that interests you
- Keep two distinct wardrobes to ease the mental transition between professional and casual settings
- A lack of time and effort limits leads to the serious issue of workaholism

How to Establish Limits in a Romantic Relationship

When it comes to setting boundaries, romantic relationships may be the most difficult. Contrary to what movies would have you believe, it is not always healthy to give your entire being to another person, no matter how romantic it may seem. Having said that, you are not required to give up being you and needing your space.

Healthy boundaries are necessary for healthy relationships. They include acknowledging each party's responsibilities, frequency of meetings and other interactions, and the minimum requirements for each person to feel secure and respected. Having boundaries in your relationships keeps you from becoming overly reliant on each other.

Imagine if your romantic interest began to interfere with your professional obligations or time spent with loved ones. If this is the case, you should take a step back and consider where you want to draw the line.

The absence of boundaries in relationships most frequently shows up in three ways:

How Long Do You Spend with Each Other

Assume you and your partner spend every moment together. If this is the case, you may need to set more time boundaries.

It's critical to strike a balance between spending time with your significant other and making time for other important people in your life.

Put your best foot forward in the relationship by expressing your desire for additional alone time with tenderness and tact. This could be a statement declaring, "On Thursdays, I do nothing but relax."

Establishing Sexual and Physical Boundaries

Setting physical boundaries must also be established and respected at all stages of a relationship, especially during the honeymoon phase. Before kissing, hugging, or holding hands, ask your partner if it's okay.

It's also necessary to discuss the extent to which each individual is willing to display affection in public, embrace, or otherwise cross a physical barrier.

In a sexual relationship, it is critical for both partners to feel safe and secure so that they can express themselves freely while still respecting each other's space and needs. Agreement, privacy, communicating preferences and desires, and meeting each other's emotional needs are all ways to build a healthy relationship with another person.

Consider the following scenario. A man encounters a woman who has previously experienced sexual assault or trauma. In such a case, he may respect her personal boundaries by routinely checking in to see how she feels about various types of sexual or physical contact. Suppose she divulges how a particular event triggered her emotional state. To keep her trust in this circumstance, he must respect her boundary.

Boundaries commonly include refraining from public displays of affection (PDA) and asking for permission before initiating physical contact, such as a hug.

Maintaining Emotional Boundaries

Emotional boundaries (limits on how one person in a relationship expresses emotions to the other) are among the most challenging to establish and maintain.

How do you communicate with one another? Do you pay close attention to your spouse and their needs, or do you only consider your own needs? Where do you draw the line when it comes to topics of conversation? What sort of tone do you use when you speak? When conflicts arise, what is the best way to make amends and move on?

Examples of Emotional Boundaries

"I don't think we should have that conversation over dinner tonight."

Saying or thinking about a sensitive topic makes me feel awkward. Could we keep such information to ourselves?"

"I need some alone time to sort things out."

"That kind of name-calling is intolerable to me."

"I wish I could be the person you vent to during this difficult time, but I simply don't have the emotional energy to do so. You could talk to a psychologist, your mother, or someone else."

Creating boundaries early on keep relationships healthy.
https://unsplash.com/photos/O7sK3d3TPWQ

How to Establish Limits with Your Parents

Limits with parents are a different matter. As a teen, it can be upsetting to witness your guardian rely on you for comfort or engage in abusive behavior in your presence. Now that you are an adult, you can make your own decisions regarding how to communicate with your parents and establish boundaries.

In any case, it's critical to establish boundaries. Children of all ages benefit from knowing that they can set limits with their parents regarding intrusions into their personal space, such as when they're getting dressed or writing in their journals.

Similarly, it is critical for children to understand their parents' boundaries as well. When parents want to establish rules with their children, they may instruct them to do things like *knocking* or *asking for permission* before using specific objects around the house.

Young people may need to set limits with their parents' unsolicited advice and ideas. Parents' expectations for their children's lives, no matter how well-intentioned, may impede the development of a healthy sense of independence and autonomy.

An adult can set this limit by telling their parents that they do not want advice or criticism about their choices unless they specifically request it. They will seek assistance when they believe they require it.

How to Establish Boundaries with Your Friends

Friendship is important for your well-being and pleasure, but it can be difficult to maintain a connection without boundaries. Friends who are constantly in need of your assistance may only sometimes return the favor. To set more boundaries with your friends, you must first be willing to say "no."

If you have a strong desire to please others, this could be a very difficult situation for you. It's possible that you have a hard time saying "no" when someone asks for your help or expresses concern, even if you know you don't have the resources to help them.

Perhaps some personal effort will be required as well. Setting boundaries can be difficult if you have a strong desire for approval or a low tolerance for rejection. However, true friends recognize the value of your time and regard you as an individual.

A simple "no" does not have to be interpreted as a massive rejection or betrayal. Practicing this skill may help you to establish healthier boundaries in your friendships.

How to Define Boundaries with Friends

- Make time for yourself every week
- Set a time limit for responding to texts and phone calls from your friends
- Let others know how you feel when you're stressed, ignored, or unheard
- Instead of saying "no," try "I'll get back to you," and take some time to think about your response
- Make it known that you are working hard to achieve your own aspirations and ambitions
- Only volunteer to help friends with things you know you can do. Otherwise, suggest other ways for them to get help with the problem
- Tell them you care about them but that you need to prioritize yourself for the time being

How to Recognize and Respect the Boundaries of Others

It would be ideal to have a system to help you evaluate boundaries, but in the absence of one, you can employ a variety of strategies to remain alert and avoid crossing them. It all comes down to communication and respecting the boundaries of others.

As a starting point, stick to these three guidelines:

Look for Signals

Pay attention to social cues to learn about the limitations of others. If a person you're talking to moves back as you get closer, it means you're invading their personal space.

Possible signs that someone needs more space include:
- Avoiding direct eye contact
- Moving aside
- Limiting the conversation
- Excessive bowing or "umms" and a sudden rise in pitch
- Tensed movements such as smiling, speaking quickly, or speaking with a rigid stance or folded arms
- Grimacing
- Wincing

Be Open to Neurodiverse Behavior

Everyone reacts differently to the same cues. Some people always use the same gestures, and others may not provide any cues at all, use entirely different ones, or may simply miss the nuances in your own gestures.

People with autism, on the autism/Asperger's spectrum, or other developmental issues are frequently referred to as "neurodiverse," a more recent term for this group. They may make less eye contact than usual and have difficulty initiating conversation.

Ask Questions

Never forget the power of a simple request. You may ask a person whether it is appropriate to embrace them or if you can ask them a private question.

Setting boundaries is less about building barriers and more about strengthening your bonds with others. However, you also benefit from limits in a different way.

They may warn you about potentially dangerous behavior. We do not always follow our instincts, either because we have been conditioned to believe they are irrational or because we are not logically minded. However, recurring feelings of unease or danger may indicate abuse. Take your instincts seriously if someone continues to test or cross your boundaries.

Similarly, if you don't want to be the one who breaks the rules, ask your close friends to be honest with you about whether or not they believe you are doing so. This may feel intimidating, but it will certainly be received with gratitude and establish you as a trustworthy individual with whom to set boundaries.

Boundaries, while important for a variety of reasons, are seen differently by different people. Maintaining them does not have to make you appear hostile or aggressive. Set boundaries without feeling bad about it.

In addition to a healthy diet and regular physical activity, they are an essential component of the daily self-care we strive to achieve. There is no exception here.

Finding out what boundaries are most important to you and how to implement them will benefit your mental health.

Chapter 5: Saying No without Feeling Guilty

Why do you find it difficult to say no to others? Perhaps you're constantly trying to please everyone or are afraid of hurting people's feelings. By saying yes all the time, you'll find that you get more and more frustrated and disappointed in yourself. You could also end up beating yourself up unnecessarily. We all have obligations to our family, coworkers, and friends. These relationships are important and fulfilling, and to keep them healthy, you must make sacrifices and put in your fair share of effort. However, this does not mean that you must always try to appease others.

Learning to say no without feeling guilty is important.
https://www.pexels.com/photo/man-and-woman-wearing-brown-leather-jackets-984950/

Be alert for any signs that you are making excessive compromises or time investments. You may feel irritated, resentful, and worn out because there is so much pressure these days to put everyone else's needs before yours.

The truth is that constantly saying yes to requests from people can damage your relationship with them. To effectively love and care for others, you must first love and care for yourself. When protecting your happiness and well-being, you'll come to know when it is okay to say no without making excuses. You will have a greater positive influence on others when you make some allowances for yourself and find a balance between what you need and how to care for others. Without this balance, your life will be chaotic as you try to live for everyone but yourself. You are not shutting down or avoiding responsibility because you sat no. Rather, it is a way to reenergize yourself to give your all while concentrating on the things that matter most in your life.

You can quickly self-check people's requests to determine the best response. Look within to see if it's necessary to say yes and whether you feel comfortable doing so. What are the consequences of saying no? If the thought of saying yes makes you feel awkward, or if you don't feel responsible for saying yes, consider saying no. There are benefits to saying no, and you should focus on those benefits, especially when under pressure. No does not imply that you are an evil 0r a bad person, and accepting this realization will enable you to stand firm in your intentions. Saying no to things at the appropriate times frees you up to say yes to the things that really matter. If you state and uphold your choices, people will have respect for you and what you stand for.

Why Do People Hesitate When Saying No to Others?

People are hesitant to say no to others for a variety of reasons. You may want to avoid hurting their feelings, disappointing them, or ruining your relationship with them. Whatever your reason for always saying yes, it is related to the self-harm of blaming yourself for the shortcomings of others and the subconscious linking to the negative answer you gave. It's dangerous to believe you have control over someone else's life. Allowing people to make their own mistakes and own up to them does not imply that you care less. It means you are allowing them to grow through experience. More reasons for people to say no are discussed further below.

Saying No Could Be Uncomfortable

Yes, saying no can be challenging, uncomfortable, and unsettling. Humans naturally want to be loved and admired. People consequently believe that the only way to achieve this is to make others happy by fulfilling their requests.

You will feel genuinely relevant and good when others show that you are needed and important in their lives. To keep this feeling, you would rather upset yourself by being available whenever they require your help rather than declining their requests. Saying no, especially when you are not in the right frame of mind, is the best course of action for all parties involved because, whether you say yes or no, there is always someone else who can perform that task better than you.

The stress and anxiety of always saying yes far outweighs the discomfort of saying no. Losing yourself while trying to live for others will affect your mental health. Which is better? Should you say no uncomfortably or say yes and regret it later?

In a Bid to Avoid Conflict at All Cost

People can be offended when their request is denied, and the situation can quickly devolve into chaos. As a people-pleaser, you'd rather say yes to avoid conflict than no. While you may believe you are pleasing people, they may see you as a coward who is afraid to step on anyone's toes or upset anyone. You may be overthinking the consequences of saying no, as it might not be as dire as you think.

Avoiding conflict could also lead to making excuses for others out of pure fear of upsetting someone. Every relationship has ups and downs. A little misunderstanding is sometimes required to clarify differences in relationships. Conflict is beneficial as long as it is resolved amicably. Running away from it does not fix it. Rather, it accumulates and usually leads to an explosion. To have a healthy relationship with others, whether coworkers, friends, or family, you must be prepared to face misunderstandings and resolve them without causing further harm. It's okay to disagree to agree.

People Want to Preserve Relationships

One of the most difficult decisions is to say no to your loved ones. As a parent who loves and cares for your children, you would instinctively want to grant all their requests to show your love for them. But have you considered the long-term consequences of constantly saying yes? What if you are unable to meet their needs in the future? What if they grow up expecting everyone else to do everything they want? They can't get everything they want, which can lead to depression if you don't teach them properly, but you can help them adjust to "no" situations by helping them to understand why you sometimes have to say no.

Trying to please your friends all of the time will always stress you out and make you unhappy in your relationship. Relationships require compromise, but you need to know when to say no and stick to it. A spousal relationship can easily cause you to lose your identity while trying to please your partner. You want peace in your home, so you agree with everything your partner says. While this is sometimes necessary, you may become bitter due to losing your identity and not doing what actually makes you happy.

Every relationship should have instances where a resounding no is appropriate. You can go the extra mile to explain why you said no and offer a better alternative. Bottom line: You must work out a way to say no to your parents, children, friends, or spouse.

To Avoid Upsetting Anyone

Every human is born with an instinctive desire to have all their wishes granted, but we all know how unrealistic that is. We are more receptive to positive responses because our brains have evolved to be highly sensitive to bad news. You will eventually burn out even if you are constantly trying to please people to avoid hurting them. The best you can do is find gentle ways to say no because your tone of voice goes a long way toward soothing the situation. This chapter will teach you to say no without offending or upsetting anyone.

Change in People's Perception of You

There is a chance that your coworkers, friends, and various acquaintances will have a negative impression of you. Close friends and family may know you well and will be able to talk with you to clear up any misunderstandings. Other people who don't know you well can easily misinterpret what you mean or say, which could be your reason for saying yes to them. You want to avoid any possibility of misunderstanding. As much as it is meant in a positive way, how long can you continue to gain the approval of others at the expense of yourself? Saying no may change how people see you at first, especially strangers, but they will eventually recognize your boundaries.

Set boundaries from the start of any relationship to show people what you can and cannot take. Even if an acquaintance changes their opinion of you because you declined their request, they will understand why you had to reject their bid and will adjust to accommodate your decision.

Please don't fall into the trap of believing it's within your power to change how others perceive you. Not everyone will like you, so be confident and think your words through before saying them. If you've acted inappropriately, you need to find a way to apologize and explain your actions. You don't have to grovel. For example, "I'm sorry I couldn't assist you with carrying your bags. I have a dislocated wrist that still hurts." Keep it simple, and don't be too hard on yourself if your apology is not accepted.

Sometimes people want you to be a certain way regardless of whether or not you are comfortable with it. Remember that being yourself will lead to people liking you for who you are. You know your intentions are good, so don't worry about how others see you, especially those you barely know.

People Think Saying No Makes Them Look Incompetent

People can easily convince you that saying no to a task makes you seem uncooperative and incompetent.

Don't let your coworkers' ideology persuade you that saying no is a sign of incompetence. It's a psychological ploy designed to make you agree to anything, even against your will. Saying no doesn't mean you're too lazy to put in the effort. You are competent if you perform well and keep your commitments.

Signs of incompetence include relying on others to complete tasks, being late for meetings or appointments, exceeding budget limits or spending recklessly, or any behavior where you step beyond the bounds of your work contract. On the other hand, saying no implies that you don't currently have the capacity to handle or afford to do something.

The Good Thing about Saying No

The word "No" may initially seem negative, but it is necessary to lead a happy life. Not everyone will like you, and you can't please everyone all of the time. Your chances of forming healthy relationships will be better the sooner you come to terms with this reality. All you have to do is find the right balance between saying no or yes. No is beneficial when used appropriately, so you should use it sparingly and carefully, or you'll damage relationships, isolate yourself, develop a negative personality, and possibly miss out on great opportunities. Saying no, however, does have some attractive benefits, which include the following:

- **It demonstrates that you value your time.** When you are in a negative situation or with negative people and realize how valuable time is, you will not hesitate to say no to things you do not feel comfortable doing. Why waste time on something you would never do when you could be doing something more important? It builds your self-confidence to say no, when necessary, which benefits your emotional well-being.

- **Saying no is a sign of bravery.** It's difficult to say no without explaining why. You can choose phrases like "I am not sure, or I will think about it" to sound nicer, but people will always expect you to be specific and detailed. They want you to respond to their request with a yes. You can't always explain all your no's, no matter how hard you try. It would be best if you considered saying no as an act of bravery and self-respect.

- **No indicates that you are certain of your decisions.** At this point, you must use your ability to think quickly, assess the situation, and work out whether you need to say yes or no. You may find that you have to compromise, but constantly saying yes to other people's needs is unhealthy. Resentment that builds up from constantly saying yes damages relationships. Determine what is best for you before responding, and be proud of your decision.

- **You stand firm when you say no.** In difficult situations, only the courageous and strong-willed can say no. Some people will go to any lengths to get your approval. They will persuade, entice, and use every trick in the book to get you to say yes. This will challenge you significantly when making decisions that promote your well-being. When you encounter these people, keep repeating your initial response and maintain your stance. If you're about to give up on your decision, remember why you chose no in the first place and the joy that will come from seeing it through. You will encounter this scenario in various aspects of your life, but do not be discouraged.
- **Refusing something is a subliminal way of accepting something else.** Saying no to overworking means affirming rest and self-care. You'll have more time for productive pursuits if you learn to say no.

When You Should Say No

Saying yes is supposed to make people like you, associate with you more, and assist you in solving people's problems, but what if you lose yourself in the process? Life is about finding a happy medium between opposing forces. There are some situations where you should say no without hesitation. For example, if you are overloaded, you should say no. Accepting more work than you can handle will only make you stressed, and you won't have time for other activities that you find enjoyable. When you realize you won't be able to carry out other people's requests, say no. If you've accepted a few tasks and realize halfway through that you won't be able to complete them, it could cause you embarrassment. It is more honorable to say no, and not disappoint anyone with half-completed work. Having mixed feelings about an issue signifies that you should say no or change your reply to give yourself time to think. Listen to your gut instincts and only say yes if you are completely convinced. Say no to anyone who stands in the way of achieving your goals. Saying yes all the time will slow you down and reduce your productivity. When you have a deadline to meet, it's okay to decline additional requests until you clear your schedule. Only accept other requests if you can deliver them without impeding your progress.

How to Say No Nicely

No is a turnoff, but it can be less dramatic if said nicely. Because the other person expects you to agree without hesitation, be polite and decline, so their expectations are not raised unnecessarily. The following are some polite ways to say no.

- I appreciate this, but I can't do it.
- I would love to, but I can't.
- Thank you for the opportunity but perhaps another time.
- Sounds interesting, but I cannot commit.
- Ask me in two weeks.
- I am currently maxed out.
- I wish I could.

Alternatives to saying no are phrases or sentences that mean no but do not say it directly. It will only take a few seconds for the other person to realize you are not interested in their offer. The examples provided above are viable alternatives to saying no. You could also offer to respond to their request later if they don't mind. Being kind with your words will help to alleviate the disappointment of hearing the word no. You could explain what you can do instead of acceding to their request - for example, I can't give you my shoes, but I can tell you where you can get similar ones.

How to Say No without Feeling Guilty

Naturally, most people-pleasers or those who have it as a strong instinct will feel guilty for saying no, but you must occasionally say no to prioritize your own needs. You can do a few things to find inner peace after saying no.

- **Think about why you're saying no.** Recognize that you cannot be everywhere or do everything. Also, always saying yes does not guarantee that you'll complete the task or fulfill the request if you are stressed. People will still hate you no matter how good you are, and saying no may be in everyone's best interests.

- **Just because you said no, doesn't make you inconsiderate or selfish.** It would help if you reassured yourself of this, or you'll be easily duped into believing that saying no is evil. You can console yourself by recalling the other times you said yes for the sake of others. Although, this does not support selfish people who never compromise to please others – but rather those with legitimate reasons for saying no.

- **Remember that it is impossible to please everyone.** You can only be there within your means, which is perfectly fine. Be there for loved ones and strangers alike, but know when to prioritize your health over everything else.

- **Try to figure out why it was difficult to say no.** Was the situation so dire that only you could assist? Can you postpone the request to a later date? Were you afraid of losing a relationship or the benefits you receive from others? When you understand why you find it difficult to say no, you can apply more rational solutions to the situation. Any relationship that flounders because one person occasionally says no isn't healthy, to begin with, and you're better off without it.

- **How do people always persuade you to say yes?** Do they bully you until you give in, or do they whine until you're sick of hearing their complaints and decide to help? Do they guilt trip you into believing that a bad situation is your fault and you must take responsibility to fix it? They may also overly compliment you to make you feel good before asking for a favor. Knowing their tricks will put you one step ahead in deciding what is best for you.

- **Speak politely and calmly.** You don't want to feel bad about your tone of voice causing more harm than the impact of the no being said.

- **Allow your body language to match your words.** The person you're speaking to will look for any indication that you might change your mind, so use strong body language to emphasize what you're saying.

- **You don't have to apologize for saying no,** but if you do, keep it brief.
- **Explaining your decision can also make you feel better about it.** Explain why you said no to alleviate the tension with saying no.
- **You can offer the person an alternative.** Stick to options you can deliver.

When to Use *Maybe* as the Right Answer

Yes or no can be your response when you understand the implications of your response and are prepared to deal with them. In a situation where you are unsure whether to say yes or no, you can use "maybe" to inform the person that you have not yet decided. Respond after first thinking it through because failure to deliver can lead to people losing trust in you.

Saying no will always be more difficult if you were raised to always say yes. Learning how to decline a request or invitation without feeling guilty is essential. To live a happy life, you must learn to strike a balance between saying no and yes. Regular practice of saying no at the appropriate time will assist you in engaging in activities that bring you deep happiness. Keep reminding yourself of the dangers of being a people-pleaser. To say no without feeling guilty, consider the request before responding. A series of steps for avoiding feelings of guilt were outlined above. Take a deep breath and believe that you are a nice person regardless of your response.

Chapter 6: How to Not Give a D*mn (While Not Being Offensive)

The world is a scary place right now. Whether it's personal, local, or global concerns, there's no shortage of things to worry about. No matter where you go, some people don't like what they see and will stop at nothing to remind you loudly how much they don't like it. Because of this, people are so afraid of being judged that they will go to great lengths to avoid embarrassment or being mocked. Some people develop a fear of being assertive as a result. Having established that boundaries are necessary and that it is okay to say no without feeling guilty, it can be difficult to strike the right balance between these two factors. The key is finding the balance between caring about other people and not caring about things you have no power to change.

Finding a balance between caring for others and filtering out the negative is a form of self-care.
https://unsplash.com/photos/dvXGnwnYweM

But how can we find the right way to do that? Whether you're meeting people for the first time or hanging out with friends and acquaintances, there will be plenty of occasions when you need to be yourself—and that may not go down well for some people. Read on for some advice about not giving a damn (whilst not being offensive) and why it's beneficial for your health.

Why You Should Stop Caring

If you care more about what other people think than what you think, you're setting yourself up for failure. The world is filled with judgmental people who are quick to point out your flaws and judge you based on what they think of you. There are many reasons why we care too much about what other people think of us, but the biggest reason is that it's easy to do so. We fear being rejected by others because we know that if they reject us, it will hurt our feelings. But, in the end, does it even matter? The answer is no, and here's why.

It Can Be Extremely Detrimental to Your Mental Health

When you care too much about what other people think of you, you are prone to developing negative thoughts and feelings about yourself. You can become hyper-sensitive to what people say and do around you. You'll be more likely to avoid social situations because you may be afraid of being judged, and this can lead to feelings of loneliness and low self-esteem. Caring too much also impacts your mental health through anxiety, depression, and even self-harm.

It Can Cause Stress

Caring about what other people think can cause stress by draining your time and energy. Stress is even recognized as a workplace hazard by the Occupational Safety and Health Administration (OSHA). If you spend all your free time worrying about what other people think of you, you won't have any left to spend on the things that are important to you. You may even do things that hurt just to keep other people happy.

Stress causes the body to release adrenaline, which makes the heart beat faster and raises blood pressure. This is called the "fight or flight" response. When your body is stressed, it releases hormones like cortisol that help you deal with a threat. Stress can seriously impact one's well-being, both physically and mentally. According to the

American Institute of Stress, over 70% of Americans are affected physically and mentally. It can cause short-term symptoms like headaches and fatigue, but it can also lead to long-term consequences like heart disease and even depression. When stress becomes chronic, it can cause serious health issues and make it even harder for you to recover from an injury or illness.

You Have More Important Things to Focus on in Life

You have to ask yourself, "Why do I care so much about what other people think of me?" Maybe you care about what other people think because you want to feel accepted and included in a group. But what if the group you are trying to fit in with consists of shallow people? What if the group you are trying to fit in with consists of judgmental people who put you down and make you feel like you don't belong? Nobody wants to be in a group like this, and it's something that you shouldn't care about so much. When you care too much about what other people think of you, you are wasting valuable time and energy that could be spent on more important things in life.

It's Impossible to Please Everyone

You may try so hard to please everyone, but you'll inevitably make someone mad. People will judge you no matter what you do. There will always be people who don't like you or care too much about what you think. There will always be people who judge you without any reason at all. For example:

- You may be in a toxic relationship with a jealous person who always wants more attention
- You may be in a toxic workplace with people who make nasty comments behind your back

Every one of us is criticized for something, and there is nothing you can do about it. While we can't completely stop people from judging us, we can stop letting it affect us. You are the only person who can decide what is important enough to you to warrant defending. It's impossible to please everyone, so why are you even trying?

You Lose Your Ability to Be Yourself

Worrying about other people limits your ability to be spontaneous, take risks, and just enjoy life. It also stops you from being creative and doing the things that make you happy. And even though it feels like you're putting on a show for other people, you'll lose yourself in the process because you're holding yourself back by taking notice of the opinions of others.

Others Don't Care as Much as You Think

People are too wrapped up in their own stuff to worry about yours. They have their own problems and insecurities that take up all their mental energy. Most people are too busy trying to pay their bills, keep their jobs, and get their kids through school to care as much as you think they do.

It's Just Not That Important

Some people will like you, and some won't, and that's just a fact of life. If you want to fit in or be accepted by a certain group of people, that's fine. But you don't have to change who you are to be liked by everyone. You can be yourself and still be liked by most people. You just have to find the right people. Those who truly matter will like you for who you are, not what you drive or the hair product you use. Why don't you try to stop caring so much about other people's opinions and focus on being the best version of yourself that you can be? It's the only way you'll ever find the type of happiness you're really looking for.

How to Stop Caring

Saying no to things is hard, especially when you're eager to please and have a tendency to overcommit, but saying no strategically instead of reflexively can be liberating. It saves you time and energy and helps you focus on what's most important to you. Letting people know that your time and attention are limited doesn't make you less likable or trustworthy. It makes you more endearing and admirable. Here are some methods to help you stop worrying about saying no and being assertive so that you can spend more time focusing on the things that really matter to you.

Change Your Mindset

If you find yourself caring too much, it may be because you're trying to control everyone's opinions of you. You may want to be the person who pretends to like the same things as everyone else just so nobody judges you. If you want to stop caring so much, you need to stop trying to control what other people think. You can't control other people's opinions, and pretending to be something you're not will only end in disaster. All you can do is be yourself and hope that people will like you for it. If you find yourself caring too much, remember that nobody can read your mind. It's important to let go of the idea that you need to please everyone and learn to accept that some people will judge you regardless of what you do.

Realize Your Attachment Style and the Reason for It

Attachment styles are ways of describing how people form relationships with others. Knowing your attachment style will help you be aware of how you respond to the presence of others and the impact those relationships have on your behavior. There are four types of attachment styles, and they can be characterized as the following:

- **Avoidant** (preoccupied): Tend to avoid getting close to others and find it difficult to form relationships
- **Anxious** (dismissive): Very insecure in relationships, craves closeness, and worries a lot.
- **Disorganized** (fearful-avoidant): Feels both anxious about forming a close relationship with someone and also worried that the other person will reject them in some way.
- **Secure** (autonomous): Feels safe and confident in their relationship with another person. They can ignore minor disagreements or differences of opinion without feeling too stressed by them.

In western society, the secure attachment style is most common. Approximately 66% of people in the US have a secure attachment style, according to research published in the National Library of Medicine (2016). This type of attachment is characterized by self-satisfaction, warmth, and sociability.

Detach from What Is Not Good for You

Caring too much is like an addiction, and you can break it by detaching from what is not good for you. It could be your job, boyfriend, friends, or toxic family members that are sucking the life out of you. If you care too much, you'll be addicted to them, and they will be addicted to you (co-dependency). Once you notice the signs of addiction, you can make a conscious effort to detach from it. You don't have to end a relationship, but you do have to change your way of thinking about it. You do not have to quit your job, but you can change your attitude about it. Caring too much is often a choice, so you can choose to stop. You need to take back control of your life and make decisions that are good for you. For example, if you have negative feelings about your job, then you need to leave it.

Get Rid of Guilt and Shame by Using Affirmations

You probably know that guilt and shame aren't good feelings to have, but they are common emotions we experience when we care too much. Guilt and shame can keep us stuck and prevent us from moving forward because they make us feel bad about ourselves. Guilt and shame are based on the belief that you are bad or wrong. When you care too much, you'll often judge yourself and feel guilty or ashamed. You may judge yourself for eating something that isn't "healthy," keeping your thoughts to yourself, or not caring about something that other people care about. To get rid of guilt and shame, write down a list of positive affirmations, such as:

- I let go of the memories that make me feel insignificant.
- I give myself the space to heal.
- Forgiving myself allows me to forgive others.
- My compassion for myself is endless.
- I feel my feelings, *truly*.
- The events of my past have shaped me for the better.
- It is okay for me to move forward.
- With the past behind me, I am at peace.
- The more I forgive, the stronger I become.

Read these affirmations out loud (and believe them) whenever you experience guilt or shame.

Do Not Permit Others to Dictate What You Do

This may sound harsh, but people who care too much often let other people dictate their lives. You probably know at least one person who lives according to other people's expectations. If you want to stop caring too much, you'll have to stop letting other people influence how you live your life.

- You may not be able to change everyone, but you can stop letting certain people affect you

- You have a life to live, and it doesn't have to be according to anyone's expectations
- You are not your family, friends, colleagues, or the people you follow online
- You have your own thoughts, feelings, and desires that are unique to you

If you want to stop caring too much and other people dictating your life, you need to start being yourself. Don't worry about what others think. Say what you want and do what you like.

Reclaim Your Peace of Mind

The only way to stop caring too much is to stop letting your thoughts rule you. The truth is that we often all fall victim to our thoughts, and they can be very toxic if we don't recognize them for what they are. You may have heard the saying: "A mind is a dangerous place." It's true. The mind can be a very dangerous place. You'll find yourself letting your thoughts get the better of you and ruin your mood. We've all had negative thoughts, but when you care too much, you can feel trapped by them. You may feel like nothing can change, and you are doomed to suffer for the rest of your life. You can reclaim your peace of mind by using positive affirmations, mindfulness, and meditation. These tools will help you to avoid getting trapped in your thoughts and to stop caring too much.

Administer Self-Care Often

Caring too much could be the result of neglecting your own needs. Self-care is not a luxury; it's a necessity. If you're not caring for yourself properly, you'll find it difficult to set healthy boundaries, which will leave you feeling resentful and exhausted. So, if you want to stop caring too much, make sure you regularly take time out for yourself. This means giving yourself the attention you need. Self-care is different for everyone, so there is no right or wrong way to do it.

- Some people like to practice yoga, meditate, or spend time in nature
- Others like to read, paint, or write

No matter how you choose to practice self-care, remember that it should be something you like to do and must be done consistently.

Meditate Daily

You will experience high levels of anxiety if you care too much. This can be extremely debilitating and can leave you feeling trapped in a cycle of negativity. As soon as you feel like you care too much, you should take steps to calm your anxiety. Most people aren't lucky enough to have anxiety magically disappear overnight, so you'll need to find ways to cope with it while it persists. One of the best ways to do this is to meditate. Meditation is a great way to help you because it teaches you to become more in tune with your thoughts. By observing your thoughts, instead of getting wrapped up in them, you can learn to let go of the negative ones faster and more easily. This will stop your anxiety from spiraling out of control.

Meditation helps clear the clutter in your mind and allows you to focus on what really matters.
https://unsplash.com/photos/UXR-t8CZ1U

Stay True to Your Values

Your tendency to care too much may reflect a lack of pride in who you are. You know, the person who won't try new things because she's too scared, she'll look silly, and who always says "no thanks" to invitations because he's scared of being rejected? When you care too much, you need to remember what's important to you and make sure you're not compromising your values to please other people. If you're finding it hard to stop caring so much, it may be helpful to start writing a list of your values. This will help you to identify what's important to you and make it easier to stick to your guns when someone tries to pressure you into doing something you don't want to do.

Remain Nice and Calm When Saying "No"

Saying "no" is difficult for many people. When you're asked to do something, it's natural to feel pressure to say yes. However, saying "no" when you don't want to will only make you upset. Instead, try to remain calm and respectful when someone asks you to do something. This will help you avoid making a rash decision that could hurt both you and the person asking. In addition, remember that saying "yes" doesn't necessarily mean that you agree with everything being asked of you, especially at work. If anything, it just means that you're opening yourself up to more work and responsibility!

You can also politely decline an invitation or suggest that someone else take on a task by saying something like, "It would be great if (person) could take on this task instead because (reason). I was hoping we could finish X by Y date. Let me know if there is anything I can do!"

If you want to change your behavior, you need to learn how to say "no" without feeling guilty. Remember that you don't have to do anything you don't want to, even if your friends are pressuring you. To make it easier to say "no," start practicing being cool and calm when you speak. This will make it easier for you to detach from the guilt that might come with saying "no" and help you stop worrying about the reaction.

It's easy to get caught up in the opinions of others. Thinking more about what they're saying can take a toll on our self-esteem and confidence. When you don't care what others think about you, their opinions don't matter because they aren't worth worrying about. By thinking like this, you can be yourself, and that's what makes you unique. Be yourself, and don't let the opinions of others dictate who you are! You should also remember that everyone has their own opinion. Not everyone will agree with each other, and sometimes someone may even say something that isn't true, but it doesn't matter because that's just one person in one day.

Chapter 7: 11 Ways to Show Assertiveness with Body Language

Assertiveness is key in many aspects of life, whether it's a job interview, social gathering, or networking event. And while it may be easy to exude confidence when standing up and mingling, sitting down can be a completely different story. After all, when you're not moving around, it can be harder to project an air of calm control. So, what's the secret to appearing assertive while remaining seated? The answer may surprise you, and that is to avoid fidgeting.

Body language is a powerful tool to use when trying to be assertive.
https://unsplash.com/photos/mSzCl0H4beY

Assertiveness is widely considered a positive trait. People who are assertive are often seen as confident and in control. They're also more likely to get their way, both in personal interactions and in negotiations. But what if you're not naturally assertive? Can you still reap the benefits of this desirable quality? Assertiveness plays a big role in effective communication. It involves standing up for your rights in a respectful way and making sure that your needs are met and your opinions are heard. While assertiveness is mostly about what you say and how you say it, your body language is also part of this communication. When you're feeling confident and ready to assert yourself, keep your body language open and relaxed. That means standing up straight, maintaining eye contact, and uncrossing your arms and legs. These nonverbal cues convey that you're ready to engage and not hiding anything or trying to distance yourself from the situation. Of course, it's also important to be aware of the cultural context in which you're communicating. In some cultures, assertiveness is valued more highly than in others. In general, keeping your body language open is a good way to show that you're ready to engage in a respectful discussion. Here are 10 top tips you can learn and practice to look assertive.

Keep Your Body Straight While Standing

When we want to show assertiveness through body language, one of the first things we do is to straighten our posture. This sends a signal to others that we're confident and in control. People who adopt an "erect and expansive" posture are seen as more powerful than those who adopt a more hunched or slack closed-off posture. This is because straightening our posture makes us appear larger and more threatening to potential predators. In the animal kingdom, this is known as the "dominance display." By contrast, slouching or hunching over makes us seem smaller and more submissive. Therefore, keep your body straight if you want to convey confidence and authority. Standing up tall with your shoulders back is a good way to start.

Hold Your Head High in Line with Your Spine

Another posture to help project confidence is holding your head high and keeping your spine straight. This may seem too simple, but it actually has a big impact on how you are seen by others. According to scientists, our posture can affect our hormone levels and nervous system, which, in turn, influences our mood and behavior. For example, standing up straight with your head held high has been shown to increase testosterone and reduce cortisol levels. This combination of hormones is associated with confidence, power, and assertiveness. In addition, good posture helps us to breathe more deeply and efficiently, which has a calming effect on the body and mind. When we slouch, on the other hand, our breathing becomes shallow, and our muscles tense up, making us feel anxious and stressed.

Holding your head high also gives the impression that you are comfortable in your own skin and believe in what you are saying. This, in turn, makes others more likely to listen to you and take you seriously. On the other hand, slouching or hunching over can make you appear nervous or uncertain, which will make it harder to get your point across. So next time you need to be assertive, remember to stand up tall and proud. It may just give you the extra boost of confidence you need to get the job done.

Relax Your Shoulders

Relaxing your shoulders is also part of the body language you need to learn to appear confidently assertive. By not hunching them, you appear more confident and in control. The science behind this fact is that hunched shoulders signify *submissiveness* – and relaxation signals *dominance*. Relaxing your shoulders makes you appear more open and receptive, sending the message that you are confident and ready to engage. When we hunch our shoulders, it activates the stress response in our brains. This causes us to release the hormone cortisol, which can lead to feelings of anxiety and vulnerability. On the other hand, when we relax our shoulders, it sends a signal to our brain that we are safe and relaxed. This helps to reduce cortisol levels and promote feelings of calm and confidence.

On a psychological level, relaxing your shoulders conveys that you are comfortable with yourself and your situation. It shows that you are not intimidated and that you are willing to engage. This can be an effective way to assert yourself, especially in cases where you feel outnumbered or outmatched. You can often diffuse tense situations and come out on top by appearing calm and confident. So next time you find yourself in a situation where you need to show some assertiveness, remember to relax your shoulders and stand tall.

Keep Your Weight Evenly Balanced on Both Feet

Most people understand that assertiveness is an important quality when you need to stand up for yourself and communicate effectively to get what you want, whether it's in your personal life or career. One way to do this is to keep your weight evenly balanced on both feet. The science behind this is actually pretty interesting. When we feel threatened or unsure of ourselves, we tend to shift our weight to one foot in order to be ready to run away if necessary. This "fight or flight" response is instinctive and hardwired into our brains. However, by keeping your weight balanced on both feet, you're sending a signal to your brain that you're not feeling threatened and that you're confident enough to stand your ground.

On a more psychological level, standing with your weight evenly balanced conveys calmness and composure - two qualities that are essential and which demonstrate assertiveness. It shows that you're not frazzled or flustered and that you're capable of handling whatever situation you're in. Additionally, it can help you appear taller and more commanding - another plus when it comes to asserting yourself. So next time you need to show some assertiveness, remember to keep your weight balanced on both feet!

Sit up Straight with Your Shoulders Back and Your Chest Open

Most people know that sitting up straight with your shoulders back is good for your posture. But did you know that it can also make you appear more assertive? When you sit up straight, you are sending a message to your brain that you are in control and ready to take on the world. This posture conveys confidence and power and sends a message that you are in control. The science behind this is that when we sit up straight, we are actually tricking our brains into thinking we are more powerful than we actually are. This is because sitting up straight takes up more space, and the brain interprets this as a sign of dominance. In addition, when we open our chest, it makes it easier to take deep breaths, which helps to calm and relax the body. So not only does this posture make you look more assertive, but it can also help you to feel more confident and in control. This boost in confidence can be very helpful when you're trying to be assertive. This can be especially useful in business or other professional settings.

Of course, sitting up straight isn't always easy, especially if you're used to slouching. But it's definitely worth the effort! Not only will you look more assertive, but you'll also feel more confident and capable. So go ahead and give it a try!

Have a Steady Gaze

Anyone who's ever been in a meeting knows that body language is important. When you're trying to make a point, you want to be sure that you're conveying confidence and authority. One of the best ways to exhibit authority is to keep your eyes focused on the person you are speaking to. It sounds simple enough, but it can be surprising how many people let their eyes wander when they're speaking. By keeping your gaze steady, you convey that you're focused and engaged in the conversation. And that can go a long way toward making your argument more persuasive.

But there's more to it than just looking confident. Keeping your eyes focused also has some science behind it. A study published in NCBI by Daniel L. Schacter and Donna Rose Addis on cognition showed that we're more likely to remember things if we look at them directly. So, if you're trying to make a point that you want people to remember, keeping your eyes forward will help ensure that they do.

Of course, there are times when it's appropriate to break eye contact. Respect their wishes if you're speaking to someone uncomfortable with sustained eye contact. But in general, keeping your eyes forward is a great way to show that you're assertive and confident in what you're saying.

Why Having Eye Contact Is Important When Trying to Look Assertive

Meeting someone's gaze is vital for social interactions, but it can also be a significant tool for assertiveness. Making eye contact with someone shows that you are confident and willing to engage with them. It can also help to build rapport and trust. As well as making eye contact, it sends a nonverbal message that you are interested in what the other person is saying. If you are looking to be more assertive, making eye contact is a good place to start. Here are some tips for making eye contact in an assertive way:

- Start by making brief eye contact. You don't want to stare, but letting your eyes linger for a moment will show that you are interested and engaged.
- Gradually increase the amount of time you spend making eye contact as the interaction progresses.
- Vary your gaze between the other person's eyes, eyebrows, and mouth. This will help to keep things from feeling too intense or creepy.
- If you break eye contact, do so briefly and then pick back up where you left off.

Making eye contact can initially feel awkward or uncomfortable, but it is a skill that gets easier with practice. The next time you are in a conversation, try paying attention to your eye contact and see if it makes a difference in how assertive you feel.

Make Sure Your Arms And Legs Are Uncrossed While Sitting

One way to show assertiveness while seated is to make sure your arms and legs are uncrossed. This may seem like a small thing, but body language experts say it can make a big difference. When we cross our arms or legs, we send a non-verbal message that we're closed off and unwilling to communicate. By keeping our limbs open, we signal that we're approachable and ready to engage.

There are scientific claims to back this up. A study published in the journal Psychological Science found that students who sat with their arms and legs uncrossed were more likely to be seen as interested and engaged than those who sat with crossed arms or legs. The researchers believe that our limb-crossing behavior is rooted in a basic human need for self-protection. When we feel threatened or uncomfortable, we instinctively close ourselves off from the world around us. So, if you want to come across as confident and assertive, make sure to keep your arms and legs uncrossed.

Avoid Fidgeting

That's right - fidgeting can actually make you appear more nervous and unsure of yourself, which is the opposite of what you want to convey when trying to show assertiveness. But why does fidgeting have this effect?

Well, for starters, fidgeting is often associated with anxiety and nervousness. When we fidget, we tend to concentrate more on our movements than on the task at hand, which can make us seem scattered and unfocused. Fidgeting can also be distracting to those around us, drawing attention away from what we're saying and making it difficult for others to comprehend our message and take us seriously.

So, if you're looking to show assertiveness while remaining seated, try to avoid fidgeting as much as possible. Sit up straight, keep your hands in your lap, and maintain eye contact with the person you're speaking to. By doing so, you'll convey confidence and poise - essential qualities for asserting yourself in any situation.

Walk Around Assertively

There are a few key things to remember when walking around assertively:

- **Make sure your posture is upright and confident**

When you walk into a room, the first thing people notice is your posture. If you're slouching or hunched over, it sends the message that you're not confident or assertive. On the other hand, standing up straight with your shoulders back conveys power and authority. Good posture also makes you look taller and thinner, which can give you a boost of confidence. Even if you don't feel like the most confident person in the world, faking it until you make it can go a long way. The next time you walk into a room, stand up straight and tall and watch how people respond to you. You may be surprised at the difference it makes.

- **Take large, purposeful steps**

Anyone who has seen a movie or TV show about a tough, no-nonsense character knows that they usually have one thing in common. They take large, purposeful steps. There's a reason for this. People who take longer strides are perceived as more assertive and more likely to be leaders. There's even a term for it: "stride length confidence." Of course, simply lengthening your strides won't make you an alpha male or female. But it can help you project confidence, which is important in many situations. So, the next time you need to exude confidence, remember to take big steps. It just might give you the edge you need.

- **Keep your hands at your sides**

When we walk with our hands at our sides, it projects confidence and authority. We are telling the world that we are comfortable in our skin and are not afraid to take up space. This is in contrast to walking with our hands clasped in front of us, which can make us look nervous and submissive. When we feel threatened, our natural instinct is to make ourselves as small as possible so that we are less noticeable to predators. By keeping our hands at our sides, we are sending a signal that we are not afraid and that we are not a threat. This can be very useful in business settings or in any situation where you want to appear confident and in control. So next time you need to project confidence, remember to keep your hands by your sides.

Use Hand Gestures That Can Make You Look More Assertive

- **Point your finger**

When you want to look assertive, pointing your finger is the way to go. Not only does it convey confidence, but studies have also shown that it can make you more persuasive. Of course, there's a right way and a wrong way to do it. You'll come across as hostile if you point your finger too aggressively. On the other hand, if you point your finger too timidly, you'll seem uncertain. The key is to strike the perfect balance between the two. As with all forms of body language, it's important to be aware of your surroundings and the message you're trying to communicate. When used correctly, pointing your finger can be a powerful tool for persuasion.

- **Make a fist**

Have you ever wondered why making a fist is considered to be an assertive gesture? It turns out that there's actually quite a bit of science and psychology behind it. For starters, making a fist causes our muscles to tense up, which gives us a boost of energy and makes us feel more powerful. Additionally, when we make a fist, we subconsciously prepare ourselves for fight-or-flight mode, which means that we're more likely to respond aggressively to a perceived threat. Finally, people who make fists are perceived as being more competent and confident than those who don't. So, the next time you want to send a message of strength and power, try making a fist. It just might give you the edge you need.

- **Place your hands on your hips**

When you place your hands on your hips, it's a nonverbal way of saying, "I'm in charge here." The gesture takes up space and makes you look more assertive, which can come in handy when you're trying to make a point or get someone's attention. But why does this hand gesture have such a powerful effect?

We tend to feel more powerful and confident when we take up more space. And when we feel more powerful and confident, we're more likely to take chances and seize opportunities. So, if you want to exude confidence and authority, try placing your hands on your hips the next time you need to make a point. You may just find that it gives you the extra boost of power you need to get the job done.

Leave Space Assertively

Leaving a space assertively can be tricky, but remember that you have a right to do so. You should start by expressing your feelings and needs clearly. For example, you might say something like, "I need some time to think about this." If the other person tries to persuade you to stay, be firm and calmly repeat your request. It is also necessary to listen to what the other person says and respect their position. Remember that you do not have to agree with them, but you should try to see things from their perspective. Ultimately, the decision about whether or not to leave a space assertively should be based on what is best for you. If you feel that staying in the situation would be harmful to your well-being, then it is probably best to go.

If you find yourself in a situation where you need to assertively leave a space, there are a few things you can do to make sure you do it in a way that is respectful and clear. First, it is important to be as specific as possible about why you are leaving. This way, there is no confusion or misunderstanding about your intentions. Second, make sure to thank the person or people you are leaving for their time and hospitality. This helps to soften the blow and leaves the door open for future interactions. Finally, be sure to state your intention to leave in a firm and confident manner. This will help to avoid any conflict or resistance. By following these simple steps, you can assertively leave any space with confidence and grace.

Chapter 8: Speak Your Mind without Apologizing

Are you getting used to the dull, sinking ache in your stomach when you're asked to give your opinion on something but immediately give a well-practiced, pacifying lie instead? Is the thought of expressing your genuine feelings both cathartic and terrifying?

Well, you're certainly not the only one who feels this way. This kind of self-censorship is more common than you might think, and it's becoming more widespread along with the growth of social media.

Speaking your mind without apologizing shows that you believe in what you say.
https://unsplash.com/photos/W3Jl3jREpDY

There is a difference between holding beliefs that are diametrically opposed to the norm and being conflict-avoidant to an unwarranted extent in every situation. Being apologetic at the very thought of conflict is unhealthy for you in the long term, and you probably already know how much it can interfere with your everyday life.

In this chapter, we'll take a deep dive at the possible roots of this behavior, why it's difficult to let go, and how you can get to a point where you can be at ease when you're speaking your mind. It may feel like that's out of reach, but with some persistence, effort, and desire, you can achieve the kind of confidence that'll take a huge load off your shoulders.

Why Are We Afraid to Speak Our Minds?

Understanding what lies at the root of a problem is the first step toward solving it. Let's break down why individuals have such a strong self-preservation instinct, so much so that it disadvantages their social lives and careers. It all boils down to fear.

Fear of Losing Status

This is one of the most common reasons for self-censorship. It's easy to get along with people when there's no difference in opinion between you. However, that's impossible because no two people are the same. Even if you were talking to a clone of yourself, you would probably differ in opinion somewhere.

This fear happens all the time between individuals. There are times when two people get into an argument and come out having less respect for each other. Human beings are social creatures, and seeking approval isn't an obscure addiction. For people-pleasers, someone's obvious displeasure or disapproval can feel like a kick in the stomach.

This doesn't just include opinions that might be controversial but even extends to harmless hobbies and interests. This fear is especially prevalent in teenagers or young adults who don't want to appear weird or out of place, but it's not absent in older adults either.

For the front you put up, you sacrifice your mental health and the true connections you could be forming with people. Over time, you may feel as though your friends and family don't really love you. Rather, they love the persona you've been playing, which can adapt to appease different individuals. In fact, you are loved and deserve to experience genuine connection, but it's difficult to break the vow of silence ingrained into you.

Fear of Change

Though you may think yourself a very spontaneous and free-spirited individual, everyone takes comfort in routine. Shutting yourself up for the sake of preserving your comfortable habits is something that might bring you some short-term peace of mind but is actually harming your long-term mental wellness.

Every time we're faced with a decision that we choose to avoid, it lessens our self-control. The more often we struggle to make the "right" choice, the less likely it is that we'll do so on the next occasion. Both decision-making skills and self-control are limited resources, and they deplete fast. A study found that we start eating away at our self-control only four minutes after the decision-making process. At the 10-minute mark, a significant portion of our self-control has already degraded. This leads to mental fatigue.

Routines help us reduce stress and mental fatigue because we don't have to actively think about the actions we're going to take, and we get a "reward" for completing them. If something throws you off the rhythm you've been dancing to every day, it feels like your mental health is being threatened.

Familiarity and routine bring comfort, but sometimes you shouldn't be comfortable with certain things. You may feel that pleasing a temperamental family member or superior at work is keeping you safe, and you take that approach to other people. Of course, this keeps you temporarily safe from conflict, but you pay for your uninterrupted pattern of silence and complacency by giving up your right to self-expression.

Fear of Embarrassment or Inadequacy

If you measure the success of every interaction by the approval of others, you might feel like every choice you make can either be a "right" or a "wrong" choice. If you make the "wrong" choice, you'll expose how much you fall short, usually in intelligence. This leads to feelings of inadequacy and embarrassment.

This fear is surprisingly common in perfectionists and over-thinkers, even if there hasn't actually been an event that has paralyzed and terrified these individuals when making an error like this.

We all feel inadequate to some degree, but persistent feelings of inferiority that convince you that you have no value are not normal. This mindset can make the world seem like much more of a hostile place than it really is, making you feel perpetually unsafe.

Other Fears

There can be countless reasons why someone is afraid to speak their mind. If your situation isn't represented on this list, it doesn't mean it's less valid or unimportant. In fact, if you have a more specific fear, it's all the more important to sit down with your feelings and try to make sense of them.

The fear of speaking your mind has also been shown to be linked with other existing mental health problems, particularly anxiety. If you think your fear of speaking your mind stems from some other mental health issue, it's necessary you account for it by tackling it from the root. For example, if you have anxiety, get professional help if you can afford it, or try some self-help books to learn how to alleviate some of the signs and symptoms.

Built-Up Anger and Resentment

We've talked long enough about fear, but what about anger? After all, anger is often used as a mask for fear.

The longer you deny yourself the freedom of self-expression, the more angry and bitter you'll become. At some point, however far into the future, that anger will leak out into your everyday life, and the people around you will notice. At this point, it's not uncommon for a sudden outburst or emotional breakdown to occur.

For someone with a fear of others knowing their true emotions, this may be the exact outcome they've always tried to avoid at all costs. Anger is an emotion like any other, and it wants to be free. However, you don't want to express your anger by hurting others or yourself.

You want a deeper way of expressing that anger, and hurting someone else is just a superficial expression of anger. If you've been bottling up your negative feelings, this may come off as a relief to you. Feeling obligated to stifle your anger and bottle it up is not healthy, but there are ways of expressing your anger in a productive, healthy way. After all, anger is a sign that there's a need that's not being met.

Focus on which of your needs are not being met rather than expending energy and effort into your anger, and realize that you can only fulfill those needs.

How to Speak Up Unapologetically
You Are in Control

When we engage in extreme conflict-avoidant behavior, we become well aware of the feelings we bottle up inside. For someone with such an iron grip on making sure they don't say the "wrong" thing, you may feel like the feelings inside you are running wild.

You have a lot more of a say in how you feel than you might think. Being unable to speak your mind unapologetically is a mental block. Someone else in the real world is not slapping a hand over your mouth whenever you try to speak. The only person stopping you is you.

In Cognitive Behavioral Therapy (or CBT), there's an idea that your thoughts create your emotions. If you're always silencing yourself by default, it's because there's an automatic script running through your head whenever you decide to speak up or stay silent. These are called "automatic thoughts" because you're thinking them up automatically, with no effort at all.

The longer you've been training yourself to stay silent, the easier it is to make the decision to stay silent, as it's the path you've always taken. It's the path of least resistance. Although it leaves you frustrated at yourself, it's as familiar and as natural to you as breathing.

The relationship between the outside world, your thoughts, and your emotions is intricately interlinked. If something happens, you automatically begin to interpret the event. Your interpretation and perception of the event create your mood, not the event itself.

You're sitting in a coffee shop with a friend, and you two are chatting away. Your friend makes a sarcastic joke at your expense. You take it seriously but decide not to comment on it because you don't want to seem weak. When you go home, what your friend said eats you up inside. You've taken a chunk out of your own self-confidence and your affection for your friend.

Can you see how your perception created your negative feelings about the event? If your perception was correct, your feelings would be normal. If your perception is flawed, it puts a strain on your mind as you try to make reality and your perception of it match up. This is worsened by the fact that you're predisposed to not communicate in a genuine and authentic way.

Cognitive Distortions

If your perception of reality is flawed, this may be because of what's called a "cognitive distortion." Cognitive distortions are automatic thoughts you have that follow a negative pattern. If you're only telling yourself negative things, it's no wonder that you feel afraid to speak up all the time. Here is a list of cognitive distortions and how they can manifest as:

- **All-or-nothing thinking.** If you have a tendency to assess your qualities in black or white, you suffer from all-or-nothing thinking. This is a standard cognitive distortion for perfectionists. For example, "Because I am unable to speak up, despite my best efforts, that means I'm a pathetic loser." or, "That social interaction didn't go as well as it could have, so I'm unable to connect with others." It's difficult to exist as a human being in a world where you're either a resounding success or a total failure.

- **Overgeneralization**. This is the tendency to think that because something has happened once, it's likely to happen all the time. Humans tend to believe things that they have seen the most, which is why many people believe in tricks used on the stage and in viral videos. It's just human nature to believe that you have the most visual evidence, but it can lead you to a false conclusion. If someone talks over you, you may think, "This always happens to me. I'm never going to be able to get a word in." You probably don't get talked over *every time* you try to speak, but you convince yourself that this negative pattern will occur perpetually – and that everyone you'll meet will have an overbearing personality. This bleak outlook isn't doing you any favors.

- **Mental filter**. When you select negative aspects of social interaction and totally ignore the positive, you're letting only negative thoughts into your mind. If you keep your views hidden and hear somebody make fun of them, you think,

"That's just how all people are! Selfish, unempathetic, and unable to think from someone else's perspective!" even though throughout your life, you've likely seen people who agree with your views and support them.

- **Jumping to conclusions.** When you jump to conclusions, you conclude something you can't back up with facts. This can either be done by thinking you know what other people are thinking or assuming you know what will happen next. For example, if you're about to say something but silence yourself at the last second, you may be thinking, "I spoke my mind, and my friend stayed silent. They must think I'm wrong, and they don't like me anymore." or, "If I say this, my friends are going to hate me." In fact, you can't look into anyone's mind, and you can't know the future before it happens. Maybe your friend is too absorbed in their own thoughts and is not likely to hate you over one disagreement in opinion.

The Triple-Column Technique

The triple-column technique was developed by CBT psychologist David Burns, and it's become integral when attempting to change people's negative thinking. This technique trains you to recognize when you're experiencing a cognitive distortion and manually talk back to it until you eventually do it automatically.

Take a piece of paper and divide it into three columns. At the top of the first column, write your automatic negative thoughts. At the top of the second one, write down which cognitive distortion you think your negative thought stems from. At the top of the third one, argue your negative thought with a more rational one.

For example, say you want to be part of a workplace or class discussion. You stop yourself, and the thoughts that flash through your mind are, *"I can't say anything because they'll either disagree with me or think I'm stupid. I can never get it together during these discussions. I'm always panicking, so I'll just make a fool of myself. It's best to just stay quiet because if they hear my voice shake, I'll look pathetic."*

Each one of those thoughts should be written and responded to separately, though some negative thoughts may be comprised of two or more cognitive distortions. Let's tackle them one by one.

"*I can't say anything because they'll either disagree with me or think I'm stupid.*" This negative thought stems from jumping to conclusions and mental filtering. An example of a rational response would be, "*There's absolutely no way for me to know how others will react ahead of time. And why is their reaction bound to be negative, either disagreeing with me or thinking less of me? That's not very realistic, and people are generally polite even when they disagree with something, not to mention, someone may actually agree with me and identify with my opinion, which would earn me a potential friend!*"

"*I can never get it together during these discussions; I'm always panicking, so I'll just make a fool of myself.*" This thought is caused by overgeneralization and jumping to conclusions. A rational response would be, "*Just because I've been scared to speak in the past doesn't mean I'm bound to always panic in the future. It's a self-fulfilling prophecy because how can I get better at speaking if I never practice? Also, nobody can know the future before it happens, so it's not doing me any favors to assume the worst.*"

"*It's best to just stay quiet because if they hear my voice shake, I'll look pathetic.*" This automatic thought is caused by jumping to conclusions and all-or-nothing thinking. A rational response to this could be, "*Not many people are as cruel as to think someone who is timid is automatically pathetic, but there's no way for me to read their minds in the first place. Also, even if they do leave thinking, I'm not very good at speaking in front of others, which doesn't automatically make me pathetic. I'm just not good at something, not a total zero, and I'll get better with practice. Even if I mess up, that's a step forward.*"

You don't have to split hairs when it comes to deciding which cognitive distortion you're really experiencing, as it's not an exact science. Just pick the ones that you think your thought stems from, and that's good enough. The point is that you're not just letting your automatic negative thoughts slip by and cut you down before you've even decided to stand up. If you do this enough, you'll eventually replace your negative thoughts will more rational ones. The mental block that's stopping you from speaking your mind will be gone, and you'll be able to confidently be your authentic self.

In the Workplace

While you tackle the root of your mental block, there are a few interactions you can prepare yourself for in the meanwhile. Workplace interactions can be stressful because you may not truly know your colleagues, but there are some default interactions you're sure to encounter.

Don't be shy to replace your "I'm sorry" with "Thank you." It's a great improvement for both you and your coworkers. If you can, supplement your gratitude with actions.

There are times when you have to apologize for messing something up. This is normal, as you're only human. When apologizing, put the focus on the other person instead of yourself, and avoid saying "I'm sorry" because if you say it too often, it loses its meaning. A genuine apology should focus on what you did wrong, that you understand how it made them feel, and how you'll fix it. Empathy is key.

It may be tempting to start a conversation or email off with, "Sorry for bothering you," but don't. It needlessly makes you smaller. If you need help, it can't be helped, so don't put yourself down.

With Friends and Family

It's easier to be comfortable with people you know, but there's a greater risk of being hurt or hurting them. If you want an honest discussion with someone you care about, be selective with whom you confide. Open yourself up to them unapologetically but with a level head when you've chosen that person.

Don't hesitate or start apologizing before you've been notified you did something wrong. Automatically apologizing makes it seem as if you really did do something wrong, even if you didn't.

Express your opinions without shame, but be empathetic and keep things civil. When you catch yourself worrying about what the other person is thinking, stop it. It's impossible to guess. If you're concerned about hurting their feelings, simply ask them. It's always better to talk things out than to stay silent.

Chapter 9: Dealing with Conflict and Standing Your Ground

Ever hear the age-old adage *"If doing the right thing was easy, then everybody would be doing it"?* There's a lot of truth to this simple statement. It takes real discipline to achieve the sort of change we want to see in ourselves and the world; learning how to deal with conflict and stand your ground is never easy. You have to work hard to achieve that kind of belief in yourself and to stand up to people whom you love and whose opinions you respect. This chapter will help provide you with the necessary tools to stick up for yourself while minimizing conflict as much as possible. While you can't always have people accept your needs peacefully but with little pushback, you can expect that sort of behavior and learn how to counteract that - without beating yourself up too much.

It's important to face conflict head-on and stand your ground.
https://www.pexels.com/photo/black-couple-arguing-with-each-other-at-home-5699684/

Managing Expectations

As you steel yourself for different conflicts, the first thing to bear in mind is to manage your expectations. For one, make sure you hammer this into your head. No matter what you do, there are bound to be conflicts in life. This may be especially important for you if you're a perpetual people-pleaser who tries to evade the faintest whiff of upset. People who try their best to please others have honed this habit usually because they grew up with difficult family dynamics. Then, enough time passes in which these same kids grow into adulthood, feeling like if they constantly push their best selves forward and make others happy, then they won't have to deal with any kind of conflict.

Unfortunately, no matter where you are in life, you're bound to deal with some measure of conflict. That should be your expectation. As you get older, you'll be dealing with many different types of personalities, and each person will react differently to you in various situations. Thinking that you can bypass this very normal part of life is what can get you into a lot of trouble.

So, don't try to avoid anything. Regardless of the situation or the kind of person involved, you won't be able to escape conflict unscathed. It's actually vital for you to face things head-on and learn how to maintain your composure as you do so. Being avoidant can make things much worse and lead to a sort of snowball effect that is unhelpful in the long run. You'd be surprised by how many times you avoid one major issue and realize it's created a much bigger headache for everyone involved.

Creating Boundaries

Now that we've established some important expectations, it's time to get to the next crucial step: staying true to your values and setting boundaries. Creating boundaries is extremely hard work in many ways, but it's necessary to maintain healthy relationships with others and mutual respect in all your dealings. Without this, everything in life will feel very one-sided, and you're bound to feel railroaded at all times. So, how to go about doing this?

One thing that is helpful for you to go over and over in your head is the following mantra: *"I have the same right as others, and I am my own person.*" It's surprising the extent to which we allow others a great deal of grace but never allow that for ourselves. If you believe that you have the same rights as everyone else, the rest of the work is easier.

Of course, this is all easier said than done. To begin feeling emotionally strong enough to implement healthy boundaries in life, you'll need to work on two aspects; building your self-esteem and exercising more self-reflection. Boundaries are one way in which we take care of ourselves, but they are also a bit difficult to define since they aren't rigid structures that people can see and are naturally attuned to. They're something we have to constantly find respectful ways of highlighting ourselves.

If you have a healthy boundary, you can avoid feelings of resentment and disappointment, which often happen when you feel you're being pushed. These boundaries can take a variety of shapes, and they range from rigid to deeply porous. Needless to say, neither extreme is tremendously helpful.

Those with very tough boundaries tend to keep people at arm's length and not let others in, even intimate partners. They don't have many close relationships and, in some cases, avoid them like the plague. On the other hand, someone who doesn't set good boundaries is bound to find themselves overly involved in other people's problems, having a tough time saying no to people and pleasing others to a fault so that they can stave off feelings of rejection. The work of finding a happy medium can be challenging, but it's ultimately a rewarding process since it will help you find healthy relationships and enhance feelings of fulfillment and happiness.

Types of Boundaries and Creating an Equilibrium

There are all kinds of boundaries, from the physical and emotional to the sexual, but your work doesn't have to focus on just one area. You will need to develop a greater sense of self to accomplish the much sought-after equilibrium. Small, healthy habits can have a big impact. For example, get to know yourself better and learn to ask yourself some important questions. If you find yourself feeling really uncomfortable in a given situation, then it's worth asking yourself why. Becoming more comfortable with exploring your feelings is an excellent way to figure out the things you're happy to do - or not.

Doing the work of introducing boundaries can take some time, and it doesn't happen overnight. For one, testing boundaries can be easier to do in new relationships than in older ones. This allows you to set the designated boundaries early on, which makes it easier to work with. In that way, you can let people know where they stand with you and avoid feelings of hurt and confusion from the get-go.

Make sure to be consistent in your messaging, and don't renege on your desired boundaries - going back and forth and not setting clear lines does the exact opposite in terms of diffusing potential conflict. Furthermore, you might find yourself in a "boy who cried wolf" situation, in which the people in your life cannot take your concerns seriously. In fact, keeping things consistent will make it easier for you to reinforce your own beliefs and make your threshold tolerance well-known, thereby preventing sources of hurt in the future.

Incorporating different healthy habits can also make it easier for you to set healthy boundaries in the long run. For example, don't be shy about asking loved ones for some alone time every week - even if you only need one or two hours a week, make sure you stick to your decision and take the time for yourself. People who care about you won't find this an odd request; furthermore, spending time to self-reflect and engage in healthy habits is crucial to your overall sense of well-being.

If you need help dealing with bigger issues or find that maybe other people in your life are not taking kindly to your desire for alone time and setting boundaries, you can consider therapy. Talking to a professional about different interpersonal problems can be a great way for you to see clearly. Even a few sessions with someone with whom you're comfortable will help you problem-solve and build an excellent sense of self-esteem. Other healthy habits to consider include journaling and taking the time to do things that nourish your mind and soul. Go to a museum, take a walk, or read a good book. All in all, take time to build up your sense of self. The more attuned you are to your sense of being, the less likely you are to find yourself in situations where you feel diminished or talked down to.

In the Eye of the Storm

So far, we've covered different ways in which you can build your self-esteem, become better acquainted with your boundaries, and so on. Now, we have to cover what can be done once you find yourself in a conflict. Someone comes to you and is unhappy with a particular situation - the conversation can be even harder if it's someone you're close to and don't want to disappoint. How would you handle that while standing your ground? This section of the chapter will offer a few key tips to help.

The first skill to help you in a moment like this is to **be a good listener**. Some people end up going on the defense as soon as someone confronts them with an issue. In general, this is a bad tactic to use and can make things harder than they need to be. Being able to listen to an opposing point of view and coming from a place of empathy rather than dismissiveness or anger goes a long way. It's normal for us to want to feel like we should defend ourselves if we feel attacked, and some people could become agitated when having to listen to a concern that makes them uncomfortable. However, the best course of action is to usually sit, listen, and try to understand where the other person is coming from. People sometimes just need to be in the presence of good listeners, and that can diffuse tension fairly easily.

Of course, that doesn't mean that you just sit there, waiting to be a doormat. The next practical step for you to take is to try to **figure out the underlying issue**. Not everyone is able to explain their true concerns in a way that feels easy or straightforward. Lots of people can take a defensive stance - maybe you're the same way. So, what to do in that situation? Again, approaching the issue from a place of empathy will work wonders. Certain conflicts can arise because they stem from deeper issues in that person's life. For example, you could be dropping off your kids at school and find yourself in an argument with another kid's parents. Take a moment and figure out what's actually happening. If it's someone you know, then maybe you can ask them how they're doing. Maybe the parent is struggling at home, going through a divorce, and their fuse is shorter than usual. Or they lost someone dear to them. Taking the time to understand the person and deal with the underlying issue is an opportunity for you to show grace and compassion without short-changing yourself.

If the conflict doesn't resolve itself quickly and you're unable to diffuse tension, you may be wondering what track to take next. Most people hate this next part, but it's important for you to face the issue head-on. If the initial conflict reared its ugly head and didn't immediately retreat, then you need to set a face-to-face meeting. Some people try to go through email, text, or phone, but those are rather poor substitutes for the real thing. In fact, they often make things far worse because you can't gauge a person or try to resolve the conflict in question without picking up on their body language, facial expressions, or vocal intonations. Noticing these subtleties is necessary to resolve conflicts and keep the situation from worsening. Of course, having to sit down face-to-face requires a degree of courage, and it's not a pleasant thing to do. However, part of the work you need to do is learn to face your fears and force yourself out of your comfort zone.

Changing your mindset is another big part of the work you need to do. When confronted by something hurtful, it can be difficult not to take things personally. However, if you want to deal with the conflict without losing your cool or feeling trampled on, remember that you can get through things without getting overly defensive. It is possible to work through the argument by getting to the underlying issue without being a scapegoat for other people's problems, as long as you remain calm and listen properly.

Conversely, if you've done something to hurt someone else and are confronted with that reality, **do the grown-up thing and take responsibility.** We shouldn't want to impose standards we don't work hard to uphold for ourselves on other people. Therefore, if you've made a mistake or made someone else feel bad, then simply own up to it, and apologize. Relationships are not one-sided, and you should take time to show the care you allow for yourself to others.

Of course, the other side of the equation is that there will definitely be times in which you need to stand your ground. Don't allow yourself to be blamed completely for something in which the responsibility is shared or is at least equal. No one is the boss of you other than yourself, so don't allow them to push you around. It's definitely possible to exhibit humility and patience without becoming a doormat. It may take a lot of time to discern the difference between various scenarios and figure out how you should take ownership of the situation. In general, however, make sure that you get the hang of standing your ground and establishing correct boundaries for yourself early on. That's the only way to ensure that you're not disrespected or end up feeling torpedoed by others.

Deciding When to Take a Step Back

So far, we've covered what to do when someone confronts you - but how do you act if someone has crossed a line and you need to do the confronting? Again, avoiding the issue for a long time is not a good idea and will lead to much resentment. You should get into the habit of calling people out when necessary. There are times when you can decide to let things go. For example, do you really want to sit down with an employee who has rankled you every so often but generally does good work?

Then there are definitely scenarios in which you should speak up. If someone made a cutting remark or you were exposed to a microaggression at work, learn to calmly bring the issue to their attention and call for a meeting. Make sure to hold that meeting in private, since people don't take criticism well in front of others, and then be sure to stay calm. If the situation is particularly upsetting to you, you may feel a bit emotional, which is natural and is ok to do. But try to control your anger as much as possible since it is rarely helpful.

The next thing to do is to be mindful of your tone and posture - body language can say a lot, and taking a combative stance will not be helpful. Begin laying out your case, and remember not to get defensive. If the person in front of you begins waffling or making excuses for behavior that hurt you, point it out firmly and don't accept anything less than an apology or some course correction. You may notice that the other individual will want to drag you into an entirely different argument altogether or talk about things that happened eons ago. Don't allow that to happen. Instead, stick to your main argument and respectfully explain the issue at hand. And then give the person a chance to respond. It may be helpful to hear their viewpoint on things, and you could come to find some kind of common ground.

If, however, you find yourself in a stalemate and the person in front of you is unable to grant you the same level of respect or simply does not see things from your point of view, feel free to call it a day. Maybe this isn't the right person for you to be close to, and getting into a relationship with them may turn out to be incredibly toxic. If this is an individual you work with, learn to keep things on a strictly professional basis and keep your distance. Anyone who disrespects you and does not take your boundaries to heart is not worth your time or energy, and it's okay for you to move on.

Making an Assessment

After a painful confrontation, take the time to lick your wounds. And then, go over the situation and review how it made you feel. Taking stock of what happened can be difficult, but it's important to see what you've learned afterward. These uncomfortable situations can lead to tremendous personal growth, but only if we allow them to. It's natural to feel wounded and on the defensive after a tough conversation, especially if the resolution didn't go exactly as you had planned. Instead of beating yourself up and taking things personally, use the situation as an example of something you can be prepared for the next time something similar happens. Since we can never avoid conflict, it's best to try to learn what you can and try not to be afraid of it when it happens. Things get easier over time, and you'll find that standing up for yourself and what you believe in is more than worth the trouble.

Chapter 10: How to Be Assertive in Different Relationships

Effective communication is essential to communicate your message clearly to someone else. However, many people struggle with being assertive, especially with people they know. Still, others confuse assertiveness with aggressiveness and end up driving away the people they most care about in the name of setting boundaries. The key to effective communication is creating a balance. To make yourself understood, you'll need to have a communication style between aggressive and passive. This is where assertiveness comes in.

No matter how strong a relationship is, unless you confidently communicate your needs and boundaries, you're sure to be disappointed. Most people hesitate to be assertive with their partners, family, friends, or coworkers because they fear causing unwanted conflicts. Not everyone reacts positively to assertiveness or even accepts it. However, if you ever want to be taken seriously, you'll have to put your foot down. Assertive communication will help you do just that.

In addition to helping you communicate effectively, being assertive can significantly improve the quality of your relationships. Don't you ever get tired of misunderstandings and not being able to get your message across? With assertive communication, you can transmit your message to someone else in such a way that there's no room for miscommunication or misunderstanding. Whether you're a parent, a partner, a son or daughter, a sister or brother, a coworker, or a friend, being assertive in all your relationships will ultimately help you improve them.

Now that you've learned how to implement an assertive attitude in your life, you should understand the next best ways you can do this with the people in your life. This chapter will give you a practical guideline on how to do it. Each section sets out tips and techniques you can use to implement assertive behavior in a specific relationship, as well as some scenarios to help you understand how to act in certain situations.

Family and Romantic Relationships

Communicating assertively in your family means conveying your opinions clearly, respectfully, and directly without leaving any room for miscommunication. Clear communication is essential to have a healthy relationship with your family members and your romantic partner. Have you ever been in a situation where you tried to communicate something, but it was lost on the other person? Or, in another case, have you ever felt bad after being unreasonably aggressive while trying to get your point across to a loved one?

Passive or aggressive communication gets you nowhere, especially when you're dealing with your family. To have a good relationship with your family, whether it's your spouse, parents, children, siblings, or other relatives, you'll need to be self-confident and courageous to implement assertiveness into your relationships. It simply isn't enough to dodge them or try to get them to understand without clearly communicating your thoughts.

With family, showing assertiveness is especially difficult because you're always scared of hurting or offending them somehow. However, you should understand that while being assertive might seem too straightforward or even rude, it doesn't seem that way if you do it properly. Spending time with family shouldn't be a chore, but something you like to do. It starts feeling like a burden when you're facing conflict or disturbance. Some people are more disruptive and tend to misbehave with others, which is why it is essential to create healthy boundaries.

The best way you can be assertive with family is to gather enough strength to not lose your temper with them. There's a fine line between assertiveness and aggressiveness, which is why you have to be careful when treading this line. This does not mean you should ignore the other person's antics, even if they are making you uncomfortable, as this would be called passive behavior. What you'd need to do in the event of a conflict or misunderstanding is confront it in a clear and direct manner.

Some tips you can follow to be more assertive in family relations include:

- **Don't be afraid to speak your mind.** Communicate clearly what you want and don't want. For instance, if you're uncomfortable arguing at a family event with another member of your family, clearly tell them it's not a good time to discuss the conflict. Do not feel pressured to argue then and there. This is not what assertiveness is about. Rather, it is about what actions best align with you.

- **If someone tries to escalate or start an argument with you**, and you don't want to indulge them, then state clearly that you'd rather not have the conversation at a family gathering. This is neither aggressive nor passive. Aggressive behavior would've been to start arguing with the relative right there and then. Whereas passive behavior would've been to avoid or simply ignore their taunts or insults. Keep in mind that ignoring them is not as bad as being aggressive, and if this is what you're comfortable with, you should surely follow your instincts.

- **Dealing with insecure people.** Some people are known for their argumentative personalities and try to belittle everyone around them. The best way to deal with these people is through clear-cut, direct communication instead of beating around the bush or escalating the disagreement. These people are usually very insecure and thrive on the attention they get from their silly arguments. To assertively end an argument with them, you can say, *"Let's agree to disagree; you have your opinions, and I have mine." "Let's not further waste our time on this subject."*

To better understand how you can implement assertiveness into your behavior, especially when dealing with family, consider these scenarios:

Scenario 1:

You've had a long day at work and just arrived home. You find the house in chaos, with dirty clothes strewn all over, dirty dishes scattered across the kitchen counter, and your kids fighting over the TV remote. Your parents have left you a dozen messages asking you to get something fixed urgently at their house, and you've got work of your own to tend to. You feel overburdened, exploited, and just tired. Does this situation sound familiar?

The first step you need to take to remedy this situation is to realize whether these occurrences are frequent. When you do this, you'll also automatically become aware of the feelings you get when facing these situations. These can include:

- Feelings of tiredness, fatigue, and being manipulated.
- You often feel like you're being taken for granted, even though a lot of the household is dependent on you.
- You get angry or frustrated the moment you step into the house or try to communicate with your family members
- You're either suppressing your anger or losing your temper at the smallest things

Once you've realized how you're feeling with regard to the treatment your family exposes you to, the next step is to identify how you've allowed this behavior to go unnoticed. For instance:

- You let the kids go unpunished after they forget to tidy up after themselves
- You let yourself be the bad cop parent while your partner always gives in to the kids' wishes
- When someone loses something in the house, you're the one to find it for them instead of having them take responsibility for their possessions
- You have not directly asked for help from your kids or your partner with the household chores
- You haven't made your parents aware of your busy schedule

Finally, you need to replace your lenient behavior with an assertive attitude to make sure you're not overburdened or taken for granted.

You can do this by:

- **Clarifying your expectations from your children, spouse, and parents.** Your family members will not automatically know that you expect them to help out with house chores or to behave a certain way. Problems like these usually occur when expectations are not being communicated properly. You can do this by implementing different assertive approaches. These include:
    - Basic assertions: this should include a basic statement of what your expectations are from your family members.
    - Question assertion: this should be a question encouraging and inviting your family members to respond positively
    - Empathy assertion: this statement should convey that you're considerate of the other person's feelings but also communicates your boundaries
    - Discrepancy assertion: this statement should refer back to a previous conversation or agreement which wasn't followed through
    - Negative assertion: this should convey how you feel about a certain situation and why you see the need for change
    - Sanctions assertion: this should demonstrate that you're committed to bringing about the change you require, one way or another. This method usually works well with children.

    Once you've clarified your expectations with assertive approaches, you may start to see some changes in your family's behavior. If they're doing as you asked, you can reinforce your assertion by praising and rewarding their behavior.

As a parent, you may hesitate to put restrictions on your children. After all, you want to provide them with the best life. However, this could leave you unable to establish healthy boundaries. As a result, you struggle with controlling your children's behavior and can't even make them capable enough to clean up after themselves. More importantly, you fail to set limits when it comes to courtesy and respect for parents. If you want your kids to treat you with kindness and respect instead of throwing tantrums or rolling their eyes, you'll need to show some parental assertiveness. As you well know by now, assertiveness sets the tone for mutual respect. This is also true for a child-parent relationship. However, communicating assertively with your child doesn't mean you become excessively authoritative or don't consider their needs. Assertiveness, in this case, would be to calmly and clearly state what you want them to do. Neither passive nor aggressive behavior can help in these situations. Passive behavior would reinforce your children's unfair behavior, and aggressive behavior would ultimately push them away from you. Finally, in addition to conveying your message assertively to your children, you should also actively listen to them so that they can explain things from their point of view.

The same approach should be implemented for your parents. If you have a good relationship with them, there's no need to use assertiveness in your relationship. However, if you have judgmental, overbearing, or manipulative parents, you need to take a stand for yourself. Difficult parents believe it is their right to criticize you and demand things from you. To be assertive with your parents, you'll first need to identify your relationship with them. For instance, if you're always looking for their approval or are irresponsible, they're likely to see you as a child and treat you like one.

You will first have to work on your own behavior to change their behavior with you. Stop looking for their approval over every trivial matter; stop acting irresponsibly or recklessly when dealing with important matters. The more you improve yourself and behave like a mature adult, the more your parents will respect you. This doesn't necessarily mean that you become completely independent from your parents, but instead, you should be mature enough to confidently establish boundaries with them.

Scenario 2:

You feel like your partner doesn't listen to you. When you talk, you feel as if you are talking to a wall. They give you one-word responses and show no interest in conversing with you.

The first step you'll need to take to get out of this situation is to assess how you communicate with your partner. Are you always complaining? Or talking behind people's backs? Or do you use harsh, inflammatory words? If your conversation style is problematic, then this is the first thing that needs to go. It is possible that your partner doesn't like conversing with you because of your style and tone of voice. The wrong tone can easily make the other person lose attention, and they might not even realize that their mind automatically zones out. So, work towards avoiding complaining too much or using harsh words.

On the other hand, maybe you started whining and using harsh words because your partner never listens to you. In this case, you need to assertively communicate your feelings to your partner. To do this, you shouldn't approach your partner with another complaint or be aggressive. Instead, use the specific language techniques discussed previously in this book to ensure they actually listen to you. Moreover, you should be considerate of your partner's needs and feelings too. You don't know if they had a tiring day or maybe a miserable one. Venting to your partner is perfectly understandable. However, you should also be mindful of their mental health and needs.

Work Relationships

Professional relationships are no less complicated than personal ones, maybe even more so if you don't know how to assertively communicate your needs to the other person. Whether you're someone's boss or employee, assertive communication in your workspace ensures that you get the best, most accurate results from your colleagues. When you present your A-game assertiveness, your needs and wants are clearly conveyed to other people. Assertive communication is even more important in professional relationships since passive behavior wouldn't yield good results, whereas aggressive behavior would create problems in the workspace. Some tips for being assertive in the workplace include:

- Be direct and clear without being offensive. There's a fine line between assertive and aggressive language. Stay respectful of others, but communicate your needs clearly.
- Make eye contact with other employees and even your bosses. Body language plays an important role in showing assertiveness, as discussed in a previous chapter.

- Assertive behavior shouldn't mean that you don't leave room for anyone else's opinions or ideas. It should, however, convey your opinion in a non-negotiable manner.
- Use "I" statements to show assertiveness, especially when facing conflict. For instance, instead of saying, "Stop taking my parking space," you could say, "I feel upset and frustrated when you take my parking space, and I would appreciate it if you didn't."
- Learn to say no. Instead of beating around the bush and trying to refuse someone's request with an excuse, simply say no. This will leave no room for any persuasion from their side. For instance, instead of saying, "I don't think I'll be able to work an extra shift tonight because I'm busy with…," you could say, "No. I don't want to work an extra shift tonight."
- Practice implementing assertiveness techniques in low-risk situations instead of confronting your boss directly. Once you've got the hang of how to be assertive without being disrespectful, you can deal with any kind of situation. However, until you do, keep control of your emotions.

Here are some scenarios you can go through to better understand how to deal assertively with workplace conflicts and situations:

Scenario 1:

Your project partner on a high-priority project has been slacking off. He keeps asking you to do most of the work and makes excuses for not being able to complete his tasks. Recently, he asked you to cover for him in an upcoming meeting. You want to say no but don't want to create tension. Here's what you could do:

Ask your coworker if they could take some time out to have a discussion regarding the project. Sit him down and explain to him clearly that you cannot juggle the whole project by yourself and need him to do his part. He might try to make excuses at this point, but close down any excuses you hear. Make him understand that he's also responsible for the project and that you won't be able to complete it without his help. During this whole conversation, you shouldn't be aggressive or disrespectful to your coworker, but you should set clear boundaries on what you can and cannot do for him.

In many cases, setting up a meeting to have a discussion isn't always possible. Many people will push you for an answer right at that moment. In these cases, be sure to clearly state that you will not be doing them any favors. Make sure you make the other person understand your message and not persist anymore.

Scenario 2:

A coworker turned rival constantly talks behind your back, makes fun of every little thing you do, and interrupts your presentations with inane questions. You feel uncomfortable any time you're around them, and no matter how much you try to ignore them, they don't seem to give up.

Unfortunately, bullying isn't limited to school and is often seen in toxic work environments. Some people never grow out of their bullying tendencies and carry the toxicity into their professional lives. The best way to deal with bullies like these is to confront them in an assertive manner. Getting aggressive in an office environment is not the best idea, and ignoring the mocking insults will get you nowhere, either. You should approach this person with clear, direct, and reserved communication. Let them know that you're aware of them having a problem with you. Communicate to them in a direct yet non-aggressive manner that if their antics do not stop, you'll have to report them to HR.

Many people confuse assertiveness with rudeness. However, you don't have to be rude if you know how to incorporate an assertive stance into your attitude. Contrary to popular belief, having an assertive attitude in your relationships can actually improve the quality of those relationships. Not only will you have a stronger bond with the other person, but you'll also feel satisfied and happy with the relationship instead of keeping it all inside.

Conclusion

Often defined as the ability to express bold, confident statements without being apologetic, assertiveness is a complex social skill. Because of this, the first step in learning to be more assertive is understanding what it is and what is not. Once you've familiarized yourself with the concept of assertiveness, it will be much easier to understand why this confident behavior could be challenging for you to express. It may be difficult to speak your mind in certain emotionally charged situations. Instead of being assertive, you go into flight or fight mode. Or, you may find being bold too pushy and choose to remain polite and agreeable instead.

If you fall into the latter category, you're a people-pleaser. You're a person who feels they must put aside their voice, time, and identity, especially in challenging situations. To become more assertive, you must change this mindset. You'll also benefit from setting healthy boundaries for yourself. Drawing the lines at the limit for your time, emotional energy, personal space, moral values, material possessions, etc., is an essential skill everyone should possess, just as saying no without hesitation or feeling guilty is. It may be uncomfortable because you don't want to cause an issue within your relationships. But why should you say yes, all the time and disregard your own wants and needs?

Many people stress about saying no because they fear they'll come across as offensive. Or, they'll hesitate to express their thoughts because they don't want to seem pushy and overbearing. To preserve your relationships, you must find a healthy balance between not caring for other people's opinions and being inoffensive with yours. While this may sound complicated, it actually involves only a few steps, like uncovering why you care about what others think and finding effective ways to stop this behavior.

One of the easiest ways to demonstrate assertiveness is through body language. The way you hold and move your body during a conversation can speak volumes of your confidence. At the same time, you can leave space for others to show respect by being assertive. Having mastered this, you should move on to learning how to speak your mind without being offensive. People with low self-esteem and assertiveness skills often feel the need to apologize every time they speak their minds. This is another behavior you need to change - and this book has provided several techniques on how to do so in different areas of your life.

Once you've learned how to speak your mind in different situations, it will be easier for you to handle conflicts. Standing your ground during an argument may seem more problematic than expressing your opinion during regular conversation. However, doing it gives you the ability to show that you're in control of yourself and others aren't. Finally, you've learned how to practice assertiveness in your relationships and find the balance between being productive in all areas of life.

Here's another book by Andy Gardner that you might like

Free Bonus from Andy Gardner

Hi!

My name is Andy Gardner, and first off, I want to THANK YOU for reading my book.

Now you have a chance to join my exclusive email list related to human psychology and self-development so you can get the ebook below for free as well as the potential to get more ebooks for free! Simply click the link below to join.

P.S. Remember that it's 100% free to join the list.

Access your free bonuses here:
https://livetolearn.lpages.co/assertiveness-training-paperback/

References

Assertiveness. (n.d.). Psychology Today. https://www.psychologytoday.com/us/basics/assertiveness

What is Assertiveness? (n.d.). Managementstudyguide.Com. https://www.managementstudyguide.com/what-is-assertiveness.htm

(n.d.). Assertiveness - an introduction. Skillsyouneed.com. https://www.skillsyouneed.com/ps/assertiveness.html

Assertive communication: Examples, benefits, techniques. (2020, August 20). Healthline. https://www.healthline.com/health/assertive-communication

Ben Richardson, A. (n.d.). Assertiveness facts & statistics: [NEW 2022 research]. Acuitytraining.co.uk. https://www.acuitytraining.co.uk/news-tips/assertiveness-facts-research/

(c) Copyright skillsyouneed.com 2011-. (n.d.). Why people are not assertive. Skillsyouneed.com. https://www.skillsyouneed.com/ps/assertiveness2.html

Clyman, N. (2020, June 20). Understanding assertiveness with social anxiety: What it is and what it is not. National Social Anxiety Center. https://nationalsocialanxietycenter.com/2020/06/20/understanding-assertiveness-with-social-anxiety-what-it-is-and-what-it-is-not/

Margarita Tartakovsky, M. S. (2015a, September 3). 3 obstacles that stop you from being assertive & what you can do. Psych Central. https://psychcentral.com/blog/3-obstacles-that-stop-you-from-being-assertive-what-you-can-do

Margarita Tartakovsky, M. S. (2015b, September 7). 5 more obstacles that prevent you from being assertive. Psych Central. https://psychcentral.com/blog/5-more-obstacles-that-prevent-you-from-being-assertive

Onyeizugbo, E. U. (2003). Effects of gender, age, and education on assertiveness in a Nigerian sample. Psychology of Women Quarterly, 27(1), 12-16. https://doi.org/10.1111/1471-6402.t01-2-00002

Psychology, W. (n.d.). Why do we struggle with assertiveness? Com.au. https://www.wattletreepsychology.com.au/why-do-we-struggle-with-assertiveness/

SemiColonWeb, & tom_web_access. (2021, September 28). Being Assertive – Why is it so Difficult? Young Minds Network. https://youngmindsnetwork.com.au/being-assertive-why-is-it-so-difficult/

What is assertiveness? (2021, June 18). Revolution Learning and Development Ltd. https://www.revolutionlearning.co.uk/article/what-is-assertiveness/

10 signs you're a people-pleaser. (n.d.). Psychology Today. https://www.psychologytoday.com/us/blog/what-mentally-strong-people-dont-do/201708/10-signs-youre-people-pleaser

Ann. (2021, November 16). What makes a people pleaser? The origins of people pleasing explained. Labyrinthhealing.com; Labyrinth Healing LLC. https://labyrinthhealing.com/blog/what-makes-a-people-pleaser

Are you A chronic people-pleaser? How to stop (for good), from A therapist. (2022, October 4). Mindbodygreen. https://www.mindbodygreen.com/articles/how-to-stop-people-pleasing

Can you change your personality traits? (2017, August 16). Society of Clinical Psychology | Division 12 of the American Psychological Association; Society of Clinical Psychology. https://div12.org/can-you-change-your-personality-traits/

Cherry, K. (2021, May 13). How to stop being a people-pleaser. Verywell Mind. https://www.verywellmind.com/how-to-stop-being-a-people-pleaser-5184412

George, C. (2020, January 8). 5 signs you may be a people pleaser and how to stop. Lifehack. https://www.lifehack.org/856814/people-pleaser

Glashow, C. (2019, November 25). 11 reasons why you are A people-pleaser — anchor therapy, LLC. Anchor Therapy, LLC. https://www.anchortherapy.org/blog/11-reasons-people-pleaser-hoboken-jerseycity-hudson-county-nj-therapist-counselor

Manson, M. (2021, February 17). The guide to strong relationship boundaries. Mark Manson. https://markmanson.net/boundaries

Martin, S. (2019, August 6). Setting boundaries with yourself: An essential form of self-care. Live Well with Sharon Martin. https://www.livewellwithsharonmartin.com/setting-boundaries-with-yourself/

Pattemore, C. (2021, June 3). 10 ways to build and preserve better boundaries. Psych Central. https://psychcentral.com/lib/10-way-to-build-and-preserve-better-boundaries

Yuko, E. (2021, July 21). This is what it looks like to set healthy boundaries. Real Simple. https://www.realsimple.com/health/mind-mood/emotional-health/how-to-set-boundaries

Elliott, S. (2019, June 7). How to say no without feeling bad about it (as told by a people-pleaser). Flash Pack. https://www.flashpack.com/solo/wellness/how-to-say-no-be-assertive/

Anderson, A. R. (2015, June 1). Learn to be comfortable saying "no" or you won't be available to say "yes" when it really matters. Forbes. https://www.forbes.com/sites/amyanderson/2015/06/01/learn-to-be-comfortable-saying-no-or-you-wont-be-available-to-say-yes-when-it-really-matters/?sh=1cd23fe6636b

LaDouceur, P. (n.d.). How to say no to people you care about. Mentalhelp.net. from https://www.mentalhelp.net/blogs/how-to-say-no-to-people-you-care-about/

Gohel, A. (2020, July 9). How to say no without hurting someone feelings. Thriveglobal.com. https://thriveglobal.com/stories/how-to-say-no-without-hurting-someone-feelings/

Boyd, D. (2011, August 29). Daily life. The American Institute of Stress. https://www.stress.org/daily-life

Farah. (2021, November 2). 9 reasons why you shouldn't care what others think of you. Medium. https://medium.com/@farahable/9-reasons-why-you-shouldnt-care-what-others-think-of-you-711e73709266

How attachment styles affect adult relationships - Helpguide.org. (n.d.). https://www.helpguide.org/articles/relationships-communication/attachment-and-adult-relationships.htm

Lim, T. (2014, September 16). 10 clear reasons why you shouldn't care what others think. Lifehack. https://www.lifehack.org/articles/productivity/10-clear-reasons-why-you-shouldnt-care-what-others-think.html

Moghadam, M., Rezaei, F., Ghaderi, E., & Rostamian, N. (2016). Relationship between attachment styles and happiness in medical students. Journal of Family Medicine and Primary Care, 5(3), 593–599. https://doi.org/10.4103/2249-4863.197314

Umberson, D., & Montez, J. K. (2010). Social relationships and health: a flashpoint for health policy. Journal of Health and Social Behavior, 51 Suppl(1_suppl), S54-66. https://doi.org/10.1177/0022146510383501

Assertive Body Language. (n.d.). Changingminds.org. http://changingminds.org/techniques/body/assertive_body.htm

Baird, A. (2017, August 14). Assertive body language. Sensei. https://sensei.ie/assertive-body-language/

Hartley, M. (n.d.). How to develop assertive body language. Maryhartley.com. https://maryhartley.com/how-to-develop-assertive-body-language/

Parvez, H. (2015, May 20). Body language: Hands on hips meaning. PsychMechanics. https://www.psychmechanics.com/body-language-hands-resting-on-hips/

Thompson, M., III. (2019, January 9). How to be assertive and stand up for yourself the smart way. Lifehack. https://www.lifehack.org/819319/how-to-be-assertive

Umoh, R. (2017, August 17). How making eye contact can help you appear more confident at work. CNBC. https://www.cnbc.com/2017/08/17/how-making-eye-contact-can-help-you-appear-more-confident-at-work.html

Schacter, D. L., Addis, D. R., Hassabis, D., Martin, V. C., Spreng, R. N., & Szpunar, K. K. (2012). The future of memory: remembering, imagining, and the brain. Neuron, 76(4), 677–694. https://doi.org/10.1016/j.neuron.2012.11.001

Burns, D. D. (2012). Feeling good: The new mood therapy. Harper.

Detert, J. R., & Edmondson, A. C. (2007, May 1). Why employees are afraid to speak. Harvard Business Review. https://hbr.org/2007/05/why-employees-are-afraid-to-speak

Rosenberg, M. B. (2015). Nonviolent Communication 3rd Ed. Puddle Dancer Press.

Vohs, K. D., Baumeister, R. F., Schmeichel, B. J., Twenge, J. M., Nelson, N. M., & Tice, D. M. (2014). Making choices impairs subsequent self-control: A limited-resource account of decision making, self-regulation, and active initiative. Motivation Science, 1(S), 19–42. https://doi.org/10.1037/2333-8113.1.s.19

9 steps for dealing with peer conflict. (2019, February 18). Soundview Executive Book Summaries; Soundview Book Summaries. https://www.summary.com/magazine/9-steps-for-dealing-with-peer-conflict/?msclkid=5a41af98be141be2f54ccce8aa437be9&utm_source=bing&utm_medium=cpc&utm_campaign=L-%20%20Blog%20Dynamic%20Target&utm_term=Magazine&utm_content=Blog%2Fmagazine%20Target

Pattemore, C. (2021, June 3). 10 ways to build and preserve better boundaries. Psych Central. https://psychcentral.com/lib/10-way-to-build-and-preserve-better-boundaries

Angélica. (2019, June 6). Assertive communication with your family. Exploring Your Mind. https://exploringyourmind.com/assertive-communication-with-your-family/

Being assertive: Reduce stress, communicate better. (2022, May 13). Mayo Clinic. https://www.mayoclinic.org/healthy-lifestyle/stress-management/in-depth/assertive/art-20044644

Gaither, J. (2009, July 17). How to calm someone down. Our Everyday Life. https://oureverydaylife.com/calm-someone-down-5188465.html

Jusic-LaBerge, D. (2018, September 25). Assertive communication will help you create emotional bond with your partner. Be Here & Now Relationship Academy. https://www.behereandnow.com/assertive-communication-in-love/

Sese, C. (2015, January 13). 6 tips for being more assertive at work. Goodtherapy.org Therapy Blog. https://www.goodtherapy.org/blog/6-tips-for-being-more-assertive-at-work-0113155